A CHAPTER IN THE OPENING OF THE WEST

THE SANTA FE TRAIL

A CHAPTER IN

THE SANTA

THE OPENING OF THE WEST

FE TRAIL

BY THE EDITORS OF LOOK

RANDOM HOUSE   NEW YORK

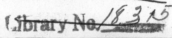

CONTENTS

A CHAPTER IN THE OPENING OF THE WEST

THE SANTA FE TRAIL

INTRODUCTION

The first white men who penetrated what is now the western half of the United States were right: there *were* golden cities at the end of the trail. Present-day San Francisco or Houston, Denver, Los Angeles or Seattle might well be one of the fabled Seven Cities of Cibola that the Spaniards dreamed of and sought. For those cities and the entire West are fabulous.

In a region that a little more than 400 years ago was unknown to the civilized world, and where only Indians lived and roamed, now flourish great industries pouring their wealth into global commerce—oil, cattle, cotton, fruits, metals, lumber, electric power, agricultural products. The settlement and development of the region has been dramatically swift. Two hundred years ago the present area of the United States supported a few hundred thousand Indians on a level precariously close to starvation. The colonists along the Eastern seaboard numbered about a million. They prospered only in a relative sense and endured innumerable privations. At the dawn of the nineteenth century the early settlers had taken 200 years to push the frontier of America westward from the seacoast up the river valleys and across the first mountain barrier of the Alleghenies to the Mississippi. In another half-century, in an unparalleled migration, they had penetrated to the Pacific. Never in history, as in that 50 years, had so large an area been settled in so short a time by so many. Today forty million Americans live in the cities and towns, on the farms and ranches of the American West.

The story of this westward course of empire is the story of the earliest travel over the great overland routes to the Pacific. For the men and women who toiled over the pioneer roads staked out at the same time the shape and character of the new nation. The history of the frontier, moving steadily over the land, became the history of the

West. The progress of the West can thus be assessed in terms of the trails and the people who traveled them, and it is in this manner that it will be told here. The tale is one of tremendous achievement, drama and action, of courage and endurance.

The great trails to the West were the Oregon-California Trail, The Mormon Trail and the Santa Fe Trail. They grew out of the earliest tracks of the buffalo and the Indians who hunted them, out of the trappers' quest for the beaver along the waterways, out of the needs of the American settlers for free and fertile land, out of their unending curiosity and restlessness, and their desire for adventure, security and wealth. These three lonely trails struck off from the Missouri frontier into the wilderness. Over them went explorers, traders, pioneers and settlers, the commerce of the prairies and the armada of covered wagons. To recount the opening of the West one has but to follow the trails, but their panorama is too sweeping to be covered in a single volume. These pages, therefore, will focus on the Santa Fe, with its color, romance and adventure. But while the subject matter of this book is the Santa Fe Trail, its significance and importance to American history can only be understood by looking at it as a part of the whole west-ward movement. For the Santa Fe, although it shares with the other routes the glamor of the opening of the West, and although it was the oldest of the trails, was overshadowed by the magnitude of the traffic carried by the other roads. It was a trade route; the others were trails of emigration and settlement. In consequence, much of the history of the West by-passed the Santa Fe Trail completely. It missed the covered wagons of the settlers, the gold rush and the trek of the Mor-mons, for example, but there is glory enough to be shared by all three trails, and the Santa Fe, when seen as part of the whole, assumes significant proportion.

At one end there was Independence, Missouri. At the other lay Santa Fe, an exotic city basking in the remoteness of the desert—a cluster of mud-walled huts. To the caravans breaking out of the moun-tains and descending the last slope to the valley it was a shining jewel, hailed with excitement and rejoicing. Josiah Gregg doubted "whether the first sight of the walls of Jerusalem were beheld by the crusaders with much more tumultuous and soul-enrapturing joy." Between Independence and Santa Fe lay nearly 800 miles of faintly marked trail, writhing its way across plains, mountains and rivers.

The trail to Santa Fe was a two-way thoroughfare of international trade. It had its wagon-trains, its ox-carts and its laden mules; but, in the beginning, they were seldom occupied by families. Westward they creaked and swayed, crammed with the precious wares of Yankee commerce; on the way back they were laden with bales of buffalo robes and beaver skins, with silver from Mexico. The Santa Fe traders had to contend with Indians, Mexicans, even with Texans, who raided their trains. Hunger and thirst, blazing heat and bitter cold were their lot. To them the trip to Santa Fe was a perilous cruise across a boundless ocean of prairie, over mountains and through rivers, amid wild beasts and among wilder men. But it ended in an exotic city and the profits were rich.

Today the Santa Fe Trail is a highway of steel and concrete. The creaking wagons that rolled painfully over the plains have made way for flashing trains, planes and autos. Santa Fe itself, dreaming in the sun of its ancient grandeurs, is overshadowed by the bright teeming cities of the Southwest, where trade, commerce and profits are on a scale undreamed of by the trail-breakers. The vast and productive empire that lies at America's command today seems to bear little relation to the pack-horse loads that made their precarious way to New Mexico—so much has sprung from so little. Although the ruts of the Trail have long sunk from view except in a few spots where they still crease the prairie, have been cemented over, covered with railroad ties or ploughed under, they still grip men's imagination today, and the story of the Santa Fe Trail, from its small beginnings to the vast development of the present, is a chapter in the story of the West.

Today as always the West is a region of magnificent scenery and awesome distances; of snow-capped mountains and barren deserts, of lush forests and rich soil, of mighty streams and pounding seacoasts; of still-untapped natural resources that overwhelm the imagination. It is a region of extremes: of heat and cold; of wealth and poverty; of lonely sheepherders and Hollywood film stars.

On the twelve following pages is a pictorial impression of the West today. Against this backdrop the achievement of the trail-breakers can be seen in magnificent perspective.

The West offers natural beauty unsurpassed anywhere in the world: the flame-colored gorges of Nevada and Colorado; the caverns of Missouri, New Mexico and Oklahoma; the glaciers of the Northwest; and the Grand Canyon of the Colorado in Northern Arizona, shown in panoramic view on these pages. In the Canyon's strata geologists read back to the earth's beginnings, hundreds of millions of years ago.

This mile-deep gash in the earth, 280 miles long, is too immense to be photographed completely, or even adequately described. Its appearance changes with the light, and ruddy buttes and walls emerge from blue and purple shadows to glow and blaze in red and gold. Colors, rock formations and clouds flow together in awesome shapes that make the Canyon one of the world's wonders.

Natural resources—among them oil—have made the West rich. Many
of its cities rising out of the plain were built on oil, "black gold" of
which the early Spaniards never dreamed. Across the broad belt of
the Southwest, oil derricks punctuate the plains and often march into
the cities themselves. Tulsa, pictured here, is the industrial capital of

a state that became wealthy through oil; and yet Oklahoma's
yearly average of 185,293,000 barrels of crude petroleum is s
by both California and Texas. Through 1945, total U. S. p
of crude oil amounted to more than 31 billion barrels, a
amount about five-sixths came from wells west of the Missi

ern rivers   and Here.
essly arid   rns are ship
shington,   ected dippi
by man,   imal. States
pt. It can   0 head of ca

America's meat
of them as large
plains and mount
tries. Cattle playe
today some 20,000,0
ranches, but the long

Symbolic of the vitality of the West, the great dams of west
harness water power, prevent floods, reclaim fertile but usel
land. The Grand Coulee Dam on the Columbia River, Wa
pictured here, is the largest masonry structure ever erected
seven times the size of the gigantic Cheops pyramid in Eg

create a fall five times as large as Niagara and three times as high; it is designed to produce over 8,000,000 kilowatt hours of power yearly. Located where a glacier once choked the river, the Grand Coulee Dam controls irrigation of the Big Bend area of the Columbia's basin; it is one of the two greatest water and power projects ever undertaken.

The West is also an agricultural country, and a wealthy one. The average value of western farms before the war was $7,929 as compared with the U. S. average of $5,518. With a great range of soil, topography and climate, the West produces every species of temperate zone and tropical crop: wheat, corn, oats, clover, alfalfa, beets, apples,

oranges, lemons, grapefruit, grapes, apricots, dates, berries. In California, the source of nearly one half of the country's fresh fruit, agriculture is the basic industry, its income far outstripping that of oil and mining together. The men shown here threshing wheat in Kansas are a part of the nine million Americans employed in agriculture.

From San Francisco, framed here under the great San Francisco-Oakland Bridge, the trade lines spread out to the Orient, linking the U. S. with lands beyond the Pacific. Before Pearl Harbor more than 300 trading houses had established headquarters in the city, and nearly 200 ship lines made it a port of call. Today the West Coast, young and ambitious, is facing the great challenge of its history. War has

poured wealth onto the Pacific slope, and a tremendous influx of people has taken place as it did before, when gold was struck. In a few years the population of California, Oregon and Washington has increased about 20 per cent and most of the newcomers want to stay. Today the future belongs to the West Coast, and to the West, as it did when the Spaniards sought the Golden Cities four centuries ago.

23

PART I The Opening of the West

CHAPTER ONE

ERA OF EXPLORATION

I N 1800, nearly two-thirds of the territory that is now the continental United States—the entire area west of the Mississippi River—was a blank on the map and was claimed by European powers. Eighty years later it was accurately charted, stable governments had been established in its political subdivisions, and more than 11,000,000 Americans occupied the region. The conquest of the American West was one of the greatest in history. The American people, standing on the frontier of the West when the Louisiana Purchase of 1803 more than doubled the area of what then comprised the United States, themselves carved the nation out of the wilderness by moving that frontier step by step across the plains to the Western Ocean. Their deeds of the next half-century were to leave an indelible imprint on the idiom and philosophy of America.

As the fateful year 1803 approached, the young Republic stood on the threshold of incredible development and tremendous expansion. To gain that threshold, pioneers had reached painfully out from the first settlements at Jamestown and Plymouth across formidable obstacles of mountain, river and forest and against equally formidable opposition by the French, who had gained control of the Mississippi at its mouth and possession of the lands bordering the mighty river.

In 1707, one hundred years after the landing at Jamestown, English colonists had pushed their settlements to the Appalachians; there, however, they appeared to be hemmed in along their strip of seacoast territory. But the English and Scotch-Irish frontiersmen were slowly pushing westward and had joined the contest for the trade with the Indians. By 1732 there were important settlements west of the Blue Ridge mountains; by 1750 the frontier had receded to the interior of

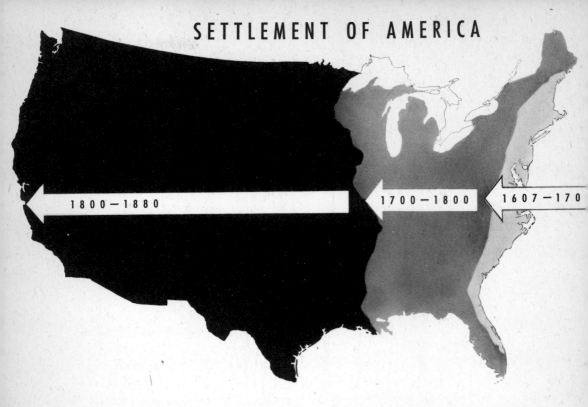

1800 — 1880   1700 — 1800   1607 — 170

Settlement began slowly, accelerated rapidly after Louisiana Purchase.

New England and along the Mohawk Valley; Pennsylvanians had pushed it up against the mountain barrier. Virginians organized the Ohio Company and obtained a tract of 200,000 acres on the upper Ohio "for making settlements and extending their trade with the Indians." The French were not slow to take up the challenge. The first shot of the French and Indian War was fired by troops under the young George Washington. With the defeat of Montcalm by Wolfe at Quebec in 1759 the war was over so far as America was concerned, and the danger of French competition was temporarily removed.

Again the frontier was on the march. Farmers of Pennsylvania, Maryland, and Virginia trekked southward in search of more and better land; in Virginia and the Carolinas the frontier advanced slowly toward the Alleghenies and the Cumberlands to lead to the first important settlements behind the ranges, in Kentucky and Tennessee. Game and Indian trails developed into roads, and rough inns sprang up to cater to the needs of travelers. But the War of the Revolution was to put a brief halt to expansion. The Kentucky outposts were ravaged, settlers were massacred, their cabins burned and their livestock stolen. The surrender of Cornwallis at Yorktown marked the end of the war in the East, but it continued in the West for another two years until news of the peace treaty put an end to the Indian raids. By the terms of the treaty of 1783 the territory of the United States was extended in the West as far as the Mississippi. By now the frontier had been pushed back from the tidewater areas across the mountain barrier; the line of settlement stood beyond the Appalachians on the border of the broad lands that now had become part of the new nation. Americans were to take possession with little delay. They had no intention of leaving these enticing acres to the Indians.

The close of the Revolutionary War was followed by great movements into Kentucky, especially from Virginia and North Carolina. Settlers marched through the wilderness or drifted down the Ohio in boats and barges. Contemporary figures estimated that 12,000 men, women and children toiled down the Wilderness Road and came down the river in 1784; in 1787 there were 30,000 of them. The early years of the young Republic were crowded with movement; a whole nation was on the march to the Mississippi and beyond. Slowly the frontier of settlement and civilization was to creep over the face of the land, gaining momentum as it went, until at last in a mad rush a tide of humanity, drawn by the lure of gold, would fling itself across the plains and over the mountains until the last frontier disappeared. In the three-centuries-long process the new nation was roughed out, shaped and hardened into its present form.

THE SPANISH EXPLORATIONS

The American frontier, in that crucial year 1803, stood on the Mississippi. What lay beyond? Relatively few Americans knew much of the vast territory west of the river; only trappers and mountain men were familiar with its wastes. Yet it comprised roughly two-thirds of the area of the United States as we know it today, and it was already rich in history before the white men beat trails of exploration and trade across it. Primitive Indian cultures existed in the Southwest thousands of years before the Spaniards, searching for the road to India that would lead them to the treasures of Asia, set foot in America. From Central and South America they had come northward to discover the riches of Mexico and to conquer the inhabitants.

In 1527 Panfilo de Narvaez, who had explored Mexico and dealt with the Mexicans, set sail from Spain at the head of a new expedition; he landed in Tampa Bay, Florida, in the following year. After taking possession of the country in the name of the King of Spain he ventured inland in search of gold, and disappeared from history when his small boat was carried out to sea off Pass Cavallo, Texas. A survivor of his wrecked expedition, Cabeza de Vaca, assumed a more important position in the chronicles of the early exploration of the West, for after

29

remaining a prisoner of the Indians for eight years he escaped and, in 1535–36, wandered westward across the North American continent. With his three companions he at last fell in with a band of Spaniards, who escorted him to Mexico City. Two years later, Hernando de Soto, Governor of Florida, set sail from Spain bent on the conquest of the land and the acquisition of its treasures to which his patent entitled him. He landed in Tampa Bay in 1539 and for four years his expedition of 600 men explored the Gulf States and penetrated parts of Arkansas, Missouri and Oklahoma. His search ended with his death at the mouth of the Arkansas; the cities of gold had failed to materialize.

Undaunted by their failure to discover gold and treasure, the greedy and credulous Spaniards continued to pursue rumors of riches in the north. They believed that in the lands northwest of New Spain lay the fabled Seven Cities of Cibola, where the inhabitants were reputed to possess golden utensils, where dwellings were encrusted with precious stones. The Spanish in Mexico were no less anxious than their kinsmen in Spain to lay claim to this fancied wealth; in 1539 Marcos de Niza, a Franciscan friar, set out through Northern Mexico into what is now Arizona, in search of these cities. Coming in sight of a Pueblo village, the bemused priest estimated it to be larger than Mexico City and judged that he had discovered the first of the Seven Cities. Hastening back to Coronado, Governor of New Galicia, the friar told his tale. The result was that Coronado, at the head of an expedition of 300 white men and 800 Indians, left Mexico in 1540 intending to take possession of the first of the wonder cities and the remainder of them in quick succession. But when they reached the "city of Cibola" they discovered it for what it was—a miserable mud village. Detachments were immediately sent out to scour the land for the other imaginary cities; one of the parties reached the Grand Canyon of the Colorado. The expedition wintered at Cicuye, east of the site of Santa Fe, and here Coronado had the misfortune to meet an Indian whom the Spaniards called El Turco, the Turk. El Turco had a better imagination than even Friar Marcos. He described to the avid Coronado the wonders of far-off Quivira, where the citizenry ate off gold plates and generally comported themselves like men of wealth and position. In the spring Coronado again got under way, across the plains of Texas, where he encountered the huge herds of buffalo that were to roam the prairie for another three centuries, and the wandering Indian tribes that hunted them. The gold was remarkable only for its absence. Convinced that El Turco had led him in the wrong direction, Coronado struck out northward with a small party of men. As he followed the Arkansas, he followed at the same time the future Santa Fe Trail that three centuries later would echo to the shouts of the bullwhackers and the

30

creak of the straining wagons. In 1541 he reached the fabled Quivira, near the big bend of the Arkansas. But here once more disappointment was his lot; Quivira was nothing but a collection of Indian huts. In a rage he had the Turk strangled and began the long march home from central Kansas—empty-handed and defeated.

Years were to pass before there was any further effort at settlement in Northern Mexico, but the Spaniards had already sailed up the Pacific Coast, discovered the peninsula of California, and entered the Colorado River; in 1542 Cabrillo sailed as far northward as San Diego Bay. Time in its march saw the Spanish frontier creep slowly northward toward the Rio Grande. At the close of the sixteenth century Spaniards had penetrated to the pueblo of Taos, had discovered mines in Arizona in the region where Prescott is now located, and the conquest of New Mexico had begun.

In 1598 Juan de Oñate, commissioned by the Viceroy of Mexico, set out from Santa Barbara, below Chihuahua in Mexico, to establish a colony in New Mexico. His ambitious expedition included 7,000 head of cattle and 83 wagons. He moved up the Rio Grande, past the spot where El Paso now stands, and at San Juan, north of Santa Fe, he settled his colony and built the first church in New Mexico. But the great plains with their mysterious treasures still beckoned to Oñate as they had lured Coronado. He roamed from the bend of the Arkansas to the mouth of the Colorado. In 1609 Santa Fe was founded by his successor, and for the next three-quarters of a century the Spaniards in New Mexico carried on their missions and their trade until, in 1680, the Pueblo revolt reduced their settlements to ruin and their people were slaughtered. It was not until 1697 that the Indians were put down by Diego de Vargas, and Spanish rule was again established. Spanish settlers began returning to the colonies, and soon they were advancing into Arizona. By the middle of the eighteenth century there were some 10,000 inhabitants of Spanish and mixed blood living in El Paso, Albuquerque, Santa Fe and their surrounding villages. But the Spaniards used the trail to Kansas as little as they could; there was still no trade to be done with the East and little reason why they should risk their lives in the dangerous Indian country. By 1770 the Spaniards had established missions in California at San Diego and Monterey, and by 1776 a settlement at San Francisco had been founded. It was to mark the northernmost extent of Spanish penetration in the West. The Spaniards, who had scoured the Western plains for gold, had at last reached their El Dorado, but they were ignorant of the treasures that lay buried in the ground they claimed. Nearly three-quarters of a century were to pass before the gold they coveted was discovered by the Americans who had, in their turn, taken possession of California.

31

And never in human history did gold pour in such a stream as from the Valley of the Sacramento. It was the ironic fate of the Spaniards to hold untold wealth in their grasp at last, and to have it elude them once again at the end of their 300 years' search.

In another sector of the great West that lay beyond the Mississippi other European powers had staked out their conflicting claims to the American empire. The French had already penetrated the interior of the continent north of the Spanish-held regions, and La Salle had taken possession for France of the vast territory of the Mississippi. In 1762 France ceded Louisiana to Spain, and by the treaty of 1763 lost to Britain all her possessions east of the river, with the exception of New Orleans. Thus America stood divided between Britain and Spain, with the river the boundary line. Meanwhile in the Northwest the fur trade had become the monopoly of the British, whose trappers of the Hudson's Bay Company and the North West Company roamed at will throughout the territory on foot and in canoes. Before the eighteenth century ended they had crossed the continental divide and entered the Oregon country. New England ship captains had by this time traded along the Pacific coast, and knowledge of the trans-Mississippi territory was increasing. In 1792 Captain Robert Gray discovered the Columbia River; George Vancouver was visiting Puget Sound, and by 1793 the Scotsman Alexander Mackenzie had traveled across Canada, crossed the divide and reached the Pacific. In 1796 the forty-ninth parallel west of the Great Lakes was surveyed by another Britisher, David Thompson, to determine whether the North West Company's posts were in Canada or the United States; he visited the Mandan Indians at the bend of the Missouri in the present state of North Dakota, and later descended the Columbia River.

Thomas Jefferson, whose interests were widely diversified, had long been fascinated by the little-known land that lay west of the Mississippi. As early as 1783 he had asked George Rogers Clark to lead a party of exploration into the Far West. The inroads of the British fur traders persuaded him that England planned to colonize the area in spite of the fact that it belonged to Spain. The Clark expedition failed to materialize and some years were to pass before Jefferson again broached his scheme.

He was convinced, however, of the existence of the *Rivière de l'Ouest* that the French had sought for so long, and the report of Captain Gray reinforced him in his belief that the Columbia River, whose head-waters he assumed to rise close to those of the Missouri, would provide

Americans and British contended for the rich fur trade of the Northwest.

a waterway to the Pacific. His lively and far-seeing mind never relinquished its hold on the problem that engrossed him, and events were now marching at a pace that even Jefferson could not have foreseen. In far-off France the interests of Napoleon, strangely enough, were rapidly converging with his own, and shortly Jefferson was to become President of the United States and in a position to put his plan into effect. In 1800, with his eye on the magnificent colonial empire of Louisiana, Napoleon coerced Charles of Spain into giving it back to him. He could not have foreseen that in three years he was to renounce it and sell it to the United States for a sum no larger than would buy a parcel of city real estate today. The news that Spain had transferred Louisiana to France filled Jefferson and his cabinet with foreboding; they had no wish to see New Orleans and the mouth of the Mississippi in the hands of Napoleon. Settlers were streaming into Kentucky and Tennessee, and the river was their main outlet. Their fears were realized when the Spanish intendant at New Orleans, acting on behalf of the French who had not yet taken over, closed the port to American products. The West was in a fever; the Federalists demanded war, the seizure of New Orleans and the settlement of the Mississippi question for all time. To avoid war with France Jefferson saw that he must purchase territory at the mouth of the Mississippi that would give the

33

Jefferson effected the Louisiana Purchase, sent Lewis and Clark to explore.

United States a voice in its control and safeguard the interests of the Westerners who had settled along its banks.

He moved swiftly on two fronts. In January, 1803, he sent a secret message to Congress asking a modest appropriation for exploration west of the Mississippi, "for the purpose of extending the external commerce of the United States," and in March of the same year he sent James Monroe to Paris as a special envoy to aid the Minister to France in negotiations seeking to purchase New Orleans from the French. Both moves were successful; the second prospered beyond his fondest dreams. At home Congress appropriated the amount requested, $2,500, and abroad Monroe had arrived in Paris to find the American Minister, Livingstone, already in preliminary negotiations. He had laid before Talleyrand the advantages that would accrue to France, now on the eve of war with England, if she divested herself of New Orleans—she would receive a large sum of money and she would be relieved of defending her possessions in America.

Monroe made his appearance in time to discover that Napoleon had offered to sell not only New Orleans but the whole of Louisiana to the United States for one hundred million francs. The American emissaries were astounded; they had no authority to negotiate such a staggering bargain. But Barbé-Marbois, the French Finance Minister, pressed them for a quick decision and warned that the offer might be withdrawn. In some trepidation Monroe completed the deal, pledging $15,000,000 for an area of land that more than doubled the territory of the United States. Napoleon was frank about the motive that had led him to sell it to America: the Louisiana Purchase, he said, "assured forever the power of the United States, and I have given England a rival who, sooner or later, will humble her pride."

EXPLORATION OF THE WEST

The Louisiana Purchase more than doubled the territorial area of the United States of 1803. In shape roughly an inverted triangle with its apex at the mouth of the Mississippi, the Purchase extended north-westward from New Orleans to include nearly all of what is now Oklahoma, most of Kansas, all of Nebraska, the eastern slope and high plains area of what is now Colorado from the Rockies eastward north of the Arkansas River, most of Wyoming and nearly all of Montana. With this immense tract added to his country, Jefferson proceeded immediately with his long-delayed plans for western exploration. To lead the expedition he chose Meriwether Lewis, who had left the Army to become his private secretary, and whom with characteristic foresight he had sent to Philadelphia the year before to study natural science. As his co-leader of the expedition Lewis picked William Clark, younger brother of George Rogers Clark, who ten years before had been approached on a similar venture.

Jefferson gave the two men explicit instructions: They were to proceed up the Missouri and find the best practicable means of reaching the Pacific by the waters that communicated with it; en route they were to make observations on latitude and longitude, climate, topography and inhabitants of the country; they were to report on the numbers and names of Indian tribes, their languages, occupations, habits and health, and the possibility of trade with them; they were to note what other nations were sending men to trade in Louisiana and the Oregon country. In May, 1804, the well-equipped party of some 45 men, of whom one-third would go only as far as the Mandan settlement in the bend of the Missouri, set off up the river. In October they reached the Indian village in North Dakota, where they built Fort Mandan as their winter quarters. Here, 1,600 miles from the mouth of the river, they busied themselves making friends with the Indian tribes. Here, also, they were aided by a French-Canadian, Toussaint Charbonneau, and especially by his Indian wife, Sacajawea, who was to become their guide and interpreter when the party reached Shoshone territory on the upper waters of the Missouri, where she had been taken captive from her home. Lewis and Clark sent warnings from their winter quarters to British trappers, advising them that the territory now belonged to the United States. In April the expedition moved on; by August they had reached the headwaters of the river and, taking to foot, they crossed the Divide and found a stream that flowed toward the Western ocean. In October they were on the Columbia, and in November, 1805, they sighted the Pacific. After wintering at the mouth of the Columbia, Lewis and Clark returned to St. Louis the way they had come. They had met with hardships, their way to the Pacific had been strewn with unexpected barriers of river and mountain, precipice and waterfall, yet they had lost only one man and they had come back with the first authentic information of the vast new land that awaited settlement. Some years elapsed before the public got an adequate account of Lewis and Clark's discoveries, but the expedition was a significant contribution to the knowledge of the Far West, and the fact that it had explored the Oregon country was later made one of the bases of the United States' claim to the territory.

Following the Louisiana Purchase there was considerable uncertainty as to the boundaries of the cession. Jefferson was handicapped by his lack of knowledge of the exact extent of the land the United States had acquired, particularly in the Southwest on the Louisiana-Texas frontier, where both Spaniards and Americans made overlapping claims. To repair the deficiencies of his knowledge he set in motion several other governmental expeditions to assemble geographical data. In 1805 Zebulon Montgomery Pike was commissioned by General James Wilkinson, Commander-in-Chief of the army, to explore the headwaters of the Mississippi, ascertain the activities of British traders and examine the possibilities of trade with the Indians. Pike found North West Company traders in possession of the territory, warned them to desist from their activities on the soil of the United States, and returned to St. Louis in the following year. Scarcely had he got back when he was sent off again on a more important mission, this time to the Southwest. Wilkinson, who had joined a shadowy conspiracy with Aaron Burr to install an independent government in the Mississippi Valley and probably to annex Mexico, desired information of the Spanish around Santa Fe.

Pike struck off, in July, 1806, along a route that marked the Santa Fe Trail for much of its extent. Following the Arkansas for some time after reaching the great bend of the river, he came across huge herds of buffalo, estimating that there were 3,000 in sight at one time. In November he was on the Purgatoire River, and he led a party up the Arkansas

Pike (left) was commissioned by General Wilkinson to explore the West.

into the mountains. It was here that he discovered on the western horizon a mountain "like a small blue cloud"; he was unable to climb it, but its name got on the maps as Pike's Peak after his death. After building a fort at the site of Pueblo, Colorado, he pressed on to explore the mountains. Although the hard winter of the high Rockies was approaching, Pike crossed the Sangre de Cristo Range after suffering severe hardships, and reached the Rio Grande, where he erected another stockade. From the moment he crossed the Arkansas he had been in Spanish territory, and it was not long before he and his party were taken into custody by a large force of Spaniards, who apparently were not unaware of the nature of his expedition. They took him to Santa Fe, where his papers were confiscated. Later he was sent to Chihuahua, examined by General Salcedo, and was returned home across Texas to the Louisiana frontier in 1807, a year after he had left St. Louis.

When Pike's journal was published it aroused tremendous interest in the adventure and profit that might be had in the Santa Fe trade, for he described the commerce carried on between Old and New Mexico and mentioned the enticing prices that yardgoods could command in Santa Fe. The mists that shrouded the mysterious West were slowly being pierced, and knowledge of vast new American resources was dawning.

Far to the northwest the horizons were being widened by the adventurous bands of fur trappers and traders, British and American, who ranged through the Rockies and the Oregon country. The mountain men, as they were called, met once a year at a rendezvous, bringing their season's catch of beaver skins to be picked up by supply trains of pack-horses sent out by the fur company. This yearly caravan pounded out the beginnings of what was to become the overland trail to the West. Such men as Kit Carson, Jim Bridger and Bill Williams knew every Indian trail and mountain pass from the upper Missouri to the Pacific, and south as far as Santa Fe. Their knowledge and experience, gained in trapping and trading, was later made use of by government expeditions and parties of emigrants whom they guided to their destinations. In 1811 John Jacob Astor, who had been buying furs in Canada from the North West Company and had become annoyed by the fact that many of the skins he had to pay duty on to bring back to New York had been trapped in territory belonging to the United States, established a trading post at the mouth of the Columbia River, where Lewis and Clark had wintered. His plan was to ship his furs direct to the Orient and trade them in China for tea and silks. The war of 1812 brought Astoria into British hands, and in the negotiations following the war joint occupation of Oregon by Britain and the United States for a period of ten years was agreed on. The Hudson's Bay Company, with which Astor was contending for supremacy in the fur trade, established Fort Vancouver on the north bank of the Columbia, near the confluence with the Willamette River, and for two decades Dr. John McLoughlin, the chief factor of the Hudson's Bay Company, held sway over the Indians and their trade. But he could not prevent them from selling to his rivals, and American traders were cutting into his territory. Even more serious inroads into his domain were in the offing; word had trickled back to the United States of the valleys and forests of the Pacific, and of the need for American settlers to people the land claimed by the United States but in possession of the British. By 1820, the frontier of the settlement, advancing from the Mississippi, had reached Missouri. The journals of Lewis and Clark had stimulated interest in the Far West, and it was now possible to travel to the head of the Missouri, hire a mountain man as guide, and proceed to Oregon via the trail of the trappers' supply caravans and the Hudson's Bay posts.

Far to the south another event took place that was to play an important part in the opening of the West. In 1822 the trader William Becknell took wagons for the first time over the Santa Fe Trail from Missouri and returned in the following spring bearing the profits of

In 1822 wagons traveled for the first time from Missouri to Santa Fe.

his operations with the Mexicans and Indians. The trade with Santa Fe boomed immediately. Calico, hardware, guns, knives, shoes were loaded into the wagons for the long trip across the prairie and the mountain range to be exchanged for silver, buffalo robes, beaver skins, wool and mules. The wealth that awaited American traders at the end of the long trek made the Santa Fe Trail one of the richest trade routes of all America.

The eyes of the restless emigrants were now turning both to the Northwest and Southwest, but always to the West. In 1832 Captain Benjamin Bonneville, the debonair soldier, arrived in Oregon at the head of a party of more than 100 men. Profiting from the experiences of the Santa Fe traders, he also had turned to wagons, and he demonstrated that they could be successfully taken through the Rockies. For the first time, wheel marks now rutted the trails of the mountain men. Captain Bonneville, acting as an intelligence officer for the United States, was the first to take wagons through the South Pass of the Rockies, and the tale of his adventures as related by Washington Irving in 1837 further stimulated the desires of those who wanted to see the West for themselves—its shining mountains, its herds of buffalo and its tribes of Indians—and have some part in the romance that appeared to be the happy lot of all who were fortunate enough to make the journey.

Soon the first venturesome souls were leaving the line of settlement on the Missouri and were making their way across the plains. The Protestant churches now began to show an interest in the West. Like the Catholic priests who had done much of the exploring in New Spain, the missionaries were to play a part in the settlement of the Oregon. In 1833 the general conference of the Methodist Episcopal Church appointed Jason Lee a missionary to the Flathead Indians of Oregon; in the following year an inter-denominational board named Dr. Samuel Parker and Dr. Marcus Whitman to study the Indians' religious needs, and by 1837 there were sixty missionaries in the Willamette Valley. Their activities were regarded with concern by the Hudson's Bay factor, who had received them courteously and generously, for it was soon apparent that, failing to make progress with the Indians, they were turning to the problems of settlement. In 1840 Lee returned from a trip to the United States with a party of 52 persons; on his visit in the East he had lectured on the need of settlers for Oregon and the desirability of seizing the country for the United States. The new settlers differed from the men of the Hudson's Bay Company, who had taken Indian wives and had made no attempt to graft the white man's civilization on the aborigine. The Americans brought their women with them, they built settlements where they intended to raise their children in American traditions, and they expected to live their lives out in their new homes. Soon they were to pour into Oregon in large numbers as the transcontinental trek began.

At the promptings of the imperialists who were clamoring for military penetration of the Oregon to ensure its seizure by the United States, the government became interested in obtaining detailed information of the land that lay beyond the Rockies. John C. Fremont, the new son-in-law of Senator Thomas Hart Benton of Missouri, who was in the van of those who advocated Oregon for America, set out on an official trail-exploring expedition in 1842. His findings were to be "auxiliary and in aid to the emigration to the lower Columbia." He was to describe the line of travel and fix the South Pass of the Rockies. In short, he was to prepare a settlers' guide-book. With Kit Carson as guide, Fremont led a party of 25 men from the Kansas River to the Platte, which he followed roughly to the site of Denver. From there he traveled northward to Fort Laramie, up the Sweetwater River and reached the South Pass, discovered by trader Jedediah Smith in 1824. He spent some time in the ranges, scaling the peak that bears his name, and returned by the North Platte and Kansas Rivers. In the following year he embarked on a much more ambitious expedition, "to examine the broad region south of the Columbia River, lying between the Rocky Mountains and the Pacific Ocean." He explored Colorado, saw the Great Salt Lake, visited the missions in the Oregon country, and was cordially received by Dr. McLoughlin at Fort Vancouver, where he replenished his supplies. Turning southward into Nevada past the neighborhood of the site of Carson City, he found that his food was dwindling rapidly and decided to cross the Sierras into California although it was now mid-winter. In March, 1844, the party arrived at Sutter's Fort, on the Sacramento River.

After rest and re-outfitting, Fremont journeyed south along the San Joaquin Valley and turned eastward over the Old Spanish Trail. He visited Utah Lake and crossed Green River, which he called the Colorado, in Brown's Park. He reached the upper Arkansas River, descended that stream to Bent's Fort, and from there followed the Santa Fe Trail to Independence. He arrived in St. Louis in August, 1844.

CHAPTER TWO

IN THE 1840's A TIDE OF SETTLEMENT
SWEPT WESTWARD FROM THE MISSISSIPPI
ALONG THE GREAT OVERLAND TRAILS.
THE BUILDING OF THE WEST HAD BEGUN.

MANIFEST DESTINY

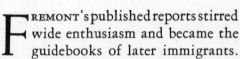

FREMONT's published reports stirred wide enthusiasm and became the guidebooks of later immigrants. The "Roaring Forties" had arrived, territorial expansion was the all-consuming desire of Americans, and "manifest destiny" was the watchword of the country as a tide of humanity swept across the land from the Mississippi. The plains had been traversed and it had become apparent that no considerations of a permanent Indian territory would be allowed to stand in the way of further settlement. The "Great American Desert" had become a meaningless label on the map. The Far West took on new significance. Once again America was to be on the march, again the frontier that had halted on the Missouri, on the edge of what had been thought to be an arid desert fit only for wandering Indian tribes, was to be displaced. The wheels of countless wagons were to mark the great overland trails across the plains and mountains from the Missouri to the Pacific, and the passage of hundreds of thousands of immigrants was to leave marks on the land that stand to this day as a monument to their courage and endurance.

The settlers who in the 1820's had arrived on the Missouri found the familiar country coming to an abrupt end. The forests through which they had fought their way from the east had disappeared, and before them stretched the prairie, limitless as the ocean. It had not occurred to them that it was land already cleared and awaiting their crops; it had appeared a barren wasteland that could not support a tree, so they had called it a desert and let the Indians have it. But the news that was now reaching them from trappers, missionaries, explorers and through government reports stirred the bolder frontiersmen to pull up stakes, load their wagons, and head out for Oregon and California.

From Independence, accessible by water, the trails struck off westward.

This westward movement was unlike any that had preceded it. The restless Americans who had been crowding the frontier halfway across the continent now faced far more difficult tasks than had ever confronted them before. The early settlers had moved at most only a few hundred miles from their starting points. Where the roads were not plainly marked and passable the waterways were deep and accessible; and in the later years they moved through partially settled areas, where aid and advice were plentiful en route. But from the Missouri to the Pacific there stretched 2,000 miles of prairie and mountain, the road was but a fitfully marked trail of wagon ruts, there were no settlements along the route where they could gain shelter, advice and encouragement, and the journey was to take from three to four months. Added to these hazards were the dangers from Indians, stampedes of cattle and of buffaloes, floods, prairie fires and sandstorms; the perils of hunger and thirst, of blazing heat and bitter cold. Little wonder that the trail of the covered wagon is strewn with the debris of failure, or that so many perished in their search for the promised land.

OREGON, MORMONS AND THE SANTA FE

Independence, Missouri, the eastern terminus of the Santa Fe Trail, over which the trade with Mexico was carried, became the favorite outfitting place rather than St. Louis, since the emigrants could save 250 miles of travel over poor roads by ascending the Missouri River to this point, where it takes a bend to the north. The Oregon Trail went by way of the Kansas River to the Platte, to Fort Laramie, up the Sweetwater River, over the South Pass of the Rockies, along the Snake River and thence down the Columbia. But no mere recital of place names or description of territory through which the caravans beat the path to the Pacific can convey the magnitude of the task to which the emigrants had committed themselves. The letters, diaries and memoirs of those who traveled the trail have told the moving story of their sufferings and sorrows. Their livestock stampeded for unaccountable reasons, they were attacked by Indians, their children fell to their deaths under the iron-shod wagon wheels, men went mad from heat and thirst, cholera struck like lightning, and the trail was marked by lonely graves. In 1843 the wagons gathered in the Missouri town for the "great migration" to Oregon; they left in May, and it was not until November that the weary party arrived in the Willamette Valley. Like those who had arrived before them, they were aided by the chief factor of the Hudson's Bay Company; the good doctor extended credit at the company commissary to the straitened immigrants, although he was well aware that in thus encouraging settlement he was failing to protect the company's interests. In the following year 1,400 settlers arrived and by 1845, when more than 3,000 immigrants entered the Oregon country, provisional government had been established by the Americans. Dr. McLoughlin's usefulness to the Hudson's Bay Company had come to an end, and he was obliged to resign his post. He became an American citizen, but his later years were unhappy because many of the settlers whom he had helped failed to pay their debts, and his own land claim was not recognized until after his death.

The Americans in Oregon now far outnumbered the British inhabitants and they petitioned Congress to establish territorial government. The expansionists clamored for the occupation of the whole of the territory, and Polk's campaign slogan, "fifty-four forty or fight," made war with Britain seem inevitable. The negotiations that had begun thirty years earlier were concluded in 1846 when the British retreated from their insistence on the Columbia River as the boundary, and the two nations compromised on the 49th parallel, thus adding more than 280,000 square miles to the territory of the United States. By the Oregon Treaty she gained what are now the states of Washington, Oregon and Idaho, part of Montana and part of Wyoming.

Of the migrations to the Far West the hegira of the Mormons was unique. Unable to live at peace with their neighbors in Missouri, many of them moved first to Illinois to found their new colony at Nauvoo. But the people of Illinois were as determined to rid themselves of this unwelcome sect as had been the Missourians, and after the murder of the prophet Joseph Smith, Brigham Young decided that the church must find refuge beyond the Rockies. Thus the Mormon Trail to the valley of the Great Salt Lake was beaten out; it followed the north bank of the Platte, whereas the Oregon emigrants had in the main stuck to the south bank of the river, as far as Fort Laramie. Thereafter it joined the main stream of westward traffic as far as Fort Bridger, where it branched off southwest into the mountains. Smith made careful preparations for the trek of the Latter-Day Saints. He sent advance parties ahead into Iowa to blaze the trail, and in 1846 the Mormons crossed the Mississippi. All spring and summer the trail was thronged with their wagons and livestock. The first-comers made preparations for those who followed them, establishing settlements for their accommodation and planting crops for them to reap. On their arrival at Great Salt Lake the Mormons broke the soil with missionary zeal, laid out irrigation ditches, and within a month a two-mile-square city had sprung up to await the coming of the thousands streaming across the plains.

Far to the south, the trade between Missouri and Santa Fe was opening the way to the Southwest, where Texas and California were still in other hands, quickening American interest in the Mexican possessions and bringing them within range of American politics. The news that Mexico had thrown off the Spanish yoke and was eager for trade with the United States encouraged a government survey of the Santa Fe Trail in 1825 and persuaded increasing numbers of traders that the road to quick riches lay in taking a pack horse or wagon train of goods to New Mexico. The route lay from Independence southwest through Kansas, across the Arkansas, and either through the mountains or across the desert into New Mexico. In the thirties and forties caravans rolled a trail across the land that became one of the historic roads to the Far West; the men who followed its tenuous ruts did much to dispel the illusion that the Great American Desert stood as a barrier to further expansion. In 1822 seventy men carried $15,000 worth of American goods to Santa Fe; by 1843, 350 men, of whom thirty were proprietors, took $350,000 worth of trade over the trail.

Increasing numbers of men were thus becoming familiar with the trails to the Southwest and with the vast area that still remained in Mexican hands. That area included Texas, New Mexico, part of Colo-

Brigham Young led the Mormons westward to the Great Salt Lake in Utah.

rado, part of Wyoming, all of Arizona, Nevada, and California. With American expansionism in full cry, it was unthinkable that the Southwestern quadrant of the country could long remain outside the national territory of the United States. Daily the trails were bringing American settlers and traders into and across the Mexican territories, and it would have taken more than exclusion acts to bar their westward progress. By 1830 there were some 20,000 Americans in the Texan province, and the Mexicans began to feel it was time to call a halt. Accordingly they put an end to further immigration from the United States and adopted restrictive laws against the American settlers. The consequences are too well known to require more than a brief recapitulation of the stirring and heroic events that brought Texas into the Union and resulted in the Mexican Cession of the remainder of their territory. A movement for independence began, and in 1836 the Texans adopted a constitution and declared themselves independent of the Mexican Republic. Mexican troops marched in. The Texans made their famous stand in the Alamo at San Antonio, and there the garrison was wiped out. Undismayed, the Americans rallied under General Sam Houston to meet the Mexicans under Santa Anna on the San Jacinto

On the San Jacinto River, 783 Texans under General Sam Houston fought

River. Following Santa Anna's defeat, the independence of Texas was recognized. The annexation of the Texan republic was, with the occupation of Oregon, the battle-cry of Polk's presidential campaign of 1844; Texas was admitted to the Union by act of Congress in December, 1845, and Polk, who foresaw the probability of war with Mexico over the annexation, moved U. S. troops under Zachary Taylor to the

the battle that assured their independence and a new southern boundary.

Rio Grande to forestall invasion. The Mexican army crossed the river, to be repulsed by the American forces, and Congress declared war in 1846. The American Army of the West moved swiftly on New Mexico, with California as its goal. In 1847 the Californians surrendered, and in the following year Mexico signed the treaty ending the war and fixing the United States boundary, by which another half-million square miles were added to the national territory. From Texas to Oregon, the whole vast territory of the Far West was now in American hands, the way was open to the army of immigrants soon to march into the new lands. Only the southern border of New Mexico remained indefinite, and in 1853, when the United States desired additional land to facilitate a railroad to the Pacific, James Gadsden went to Mexico to conduct negotiations. He purchased some 30,000 square miles of land on the border between the Rio Grande and the Colorado for which the United States paid $10,000,000. With the exception of Alaska, the continental area of the nation was now complete.

THE DISCOVERY OF GOLD

For ten years the nation's people had been on the unprecedented march to the West. From the East they were streaming to the Mississippi; from there they were hastening to the Missouri; and from the Missouri they were pressing on across the plains. The completion of the Erie canal in 1825 had sped the settlement and development of Western New York and Michigan; steamboats on the Ohio and the Mississippi were crowded to danger point with homeseekers. In the 1840's Wisconsin and Iowa saw them arrive in vast numbers. Two hundred settlers were estimated to have debarked daily at the lake ports in Wisconsin. By the fifties foreign immigrants made their appearance in the Mississippi Valley. Year after year the roads and waterways were filled with an unending stream of humanity. By 1860 lands bordering the upper waters of the river had largely passed the frontier stage, and twenty years had elapsed since it had been believed that one tier of States west of the Mississippi would mark the extent of the frontier. As the pressure on the pioneers grew heavier they left the frontier in ever-increasing numbers; the traffic of emigrants over the Oregon Trail continued through the forties, but heavy and continuous though it might be it was shortly to be overshadowed. By 1848 the ruts on the trail were deep, but soon new tracks were to be gouged to California, for a magic word had run like wildfire out of the valley of the Sacramento. That word was gold.

Of the emigrants who had come to the Far West over the Oregon Trail perhaps one-fourth of them had gone to California, to the colony established by John Sutter on the Sacramento River, where they rested after their long journey. Sutter had built a fort, engaged in the fur trade, acquired large herds of livestock and operated a grist mill. In January, 1848, one of his men picked up some yellow nuggets in the tailrace of a sawmill; the particles were assayed, the news of their nature leaked out, and the California gold rush was on. It came first from the Pacific Coast. In San Francisco three-quarters of the houses were soon standing vacant, business and industry came to a halt, crews left their ships in the harbor and soldiers deserted their garrisons. Governor Mason of California told of seeing a ditch less than 100 feet long from which two men took out $17,000 worth of gold in seven days. With little luck and less industry a man could make fifty dollars a day. The towns of California became communities of women; the only men who stayed behind were in jail.

It was not until late in 1848 that the magic news percolated to the eastern seaboard, but by the spring of '49 the prairies were covered with wagons. Independence was a confused scene of horses, mules, wagons, and oxen. In the market, men who had sold all their possessions were excitedly acquiring an outfit for the hurried journey to El Dorado; many had never handled mules and had little idea of the trip that lay before them. At least 35,000 prospectors from the Western States made the overland journey to the goldfields. Ships were leaving Britain, France, Germany and Holland for the long voyage round the Horn to California; at least 17,000 persons sailed from American ports for the Pacific in 1849, and by the end of the year there were nearly 250 ships in California harbors. When they reached port they were deserted by passengers and crew alike and left to go to pieces. The rush carried on through the early fifties. An excited America was full of the news of the riches that awaited the adventurer and of the vast expanse of land ready for occupation and development.

The greatest number of those who went by the overland routes chose the well-traveled Oregon Trail as far as the South Pass, west of which their paths diverged from those of the settlers. The Oregon Trail turned westward, following Snake River, below Fort Hall (Pocatello, Idaho). The California Trail left the Snake at Raft River, continued west to Goose Creek (Idaho) and met the Humboldt River at Humboldt Wells, the present Wells, Nevada. Many of the forty-niners followed the Santa Fe Trail and continued westward by various routes to the goldfields. As the nineteenth century reached its halfway mark, California had a population of 92,597. Ten years later it was 380,000. The westward trails were thronged as never before by a cross-section of the heterogeneous people of America, impelled by one reason only to make their way across the Great American Desert—the lure of gold.

This sudden growth of the Pacific coast population led to the swift development of the West, creating a demand for transportation and communication that normally would not have arisen perhaps for many years. The Californians soon became dissatisfied with the twice-monthly ocean mail service that was their only communication with the East and the rest of the world; the stage coach, the pony

51

The Pony Express linked St. Joseph and the Pacific in thirteen days.

express, the telegraph and railroad were to follow in quick succession.

Two years after the discovery of gold two stage-coach lines began operating from Independence, one to Salt Lake City, the other to Santa Fe. The former suffered from lack of capital and organization, but the latter line carried mail and passengers once a month for a fare of $150. Other pioneer ventures were succeeded in 1858 by Butterfield's Overland Mail, which provided semi-monthly service to the coast over a route principally notable for its length and indirection. The eastern termini were at St. Louis and Memphis, whence the road went to El Paso, Tucson and Los Angeles, then northward through the mountainous territory to San Francisco. The 25-day schedule called for by the contract led skeptics to declare that this project was bound to fail, but the Butterfield line carried the mail in both directions with time to spare, sometimes in as little as twenty-one days. Passenger fare varied from $100 to $200, but passengers were scarce; the journey was a killer and only the strongest could endure the rigors of jolting in a stage-coach for three weeks. Stages were soon being operated over the more direct Oregon-California Trail route by the firm of Russell, Majors and Waddell, who now conceived a dramatic plan to convince Congressional proponents of the southern route that mail could be carried faster over the trails traveled by the emigrants.

They proposed to establish weekly communication between New York and San Francisco by bridging the gap between the ends of the telegraph lines by relays of horsemen, and to carry mail between St. Joseph and the coast in thirteen days. This ambitious scheme was the pony express, that colorful episode in the life of the West. Its spectacular feats have never been forgotten. Summer and winter, day and night, the pony express riders galloped over the trail at breakneck speed between the relay stations. In 1860 they brought the news of Lincoln's election from the eastern terminal of the telegraph line at Fort Kearney, Nebraska, to its western end in Fort Churchill, Nevada, in six days. In its thrilling and entertaining contribution to the development of the West the pony express missed only one trip, and that in the depth of winter. As the telegraph lines pushed further inward the service became semi-weekly, and upon their junction in 1861 the days of the pony express came to an end. Congress had already authorized a daily-mail stage service over the central route, and a number of railroad bills were before it. In 1862 President Lincoln signed an act to construct a railroad and telegraph line to the Pacific. The pony express disappeared and the stage-coach was shortly to follow it, but for years after the completion of the transcontinental railroad the stage-coach and the freight-wagon continued to be the only means of carrying mail, supplies and passengers to many sections of the Far West. In the spring of 1869 the Union Pacific, building from the East, and the Central Pacific, moving from the coast, met at Promontory, Utah, north of the Great Salt Lake, and the two roads were joined in one great trunk line spanning the continent.

In its wake the railroad had brought a new civilization to the West—the rail-end towns of the construction gangs, peopled by tough, hard-living laborers and the hangers-on who made their living off them. Some of the shanty-towns were short-lived hot-spots of tents, false-front saloons and gambling joints. When the railroad moved on the community followed it, to establish itself in a new location for another brief stay. Dirty and dangerous, most of the terminal towns were thus successively erased from the map of the West, but a few of them, such as Cheyenne, Laramie and Reno, lingered on to become settled communities that soon got over their boisterous beginnings. Only the plains remained now as the last frontier of America, and soon the immense buffalo herds were to be exterminated and the Indians who peopled the prairies restricted to reservations. Cattle-raising was to become the new bonanza of the frontier until the open ranges in their turn were broken up by the entry of the farmer. When the nineteenth century entered its last decade he had carried his frontier into almost every corner. In 1860 there had been 1,364,000 people living

Life on the frontier was important in shaping American character.

54

west of the first tier of States west of the Mississippi. Thirty years later the population of the same area was more than 8,686,000. The pioneer phase of settlement was ended. The frontier line had disappeared. The West had been opened.

The frontier, ever beckoning and receding, has been the decisive factor in the shaping of America and the development of her people. Until it vanished in the last decade of the century, when fingers of settlement probed the last uninhabited areas, it stamped its imprint on all who took part in the westward movement and molded their diverse elements into a composite American people. Its influences were tangible, far-reaching and permanent; they are to be found today in the existence of American nationality, in the strength of our democratic ideals and institutions, in the unique character of our people. But those who lived in the stirring days of westward expansion had no thought for a future except their own; they would have been amazed and scornful if they had been hailed as empire-builders. They took no such long view of themselves. The millions who took to the trails were impelled by restlessness, the desire for personal liberty and the lure of adventure. What they were seeking was free and fertile land; later they sought gold. But the hunters and trappers, the pioneer farmers and immigrants, the miners and cowboys had no time to consider the idea that they might be making a nation out of the wilderness, even if the thought had struck them. They were caught up in the tremendous surge of the times. Events were moving too fast in their lives to permit of introspection. They were men of action, self-willed, headstrong, confident and aggressive, and they were too busy at the job of living to attempt to evaluate their work. It was to be left to historians of a later age to formulate the thesis that the history of America was the history of her westward expansion and that the frontier, the stage on which the drama had been unfolded in its many acts, explained her development.

But the influence of the frontier on American history was great. Life on the frontier was the culmination of the idealist's search for new opportunity, for a real equality and for security for one's self and children. There was a social democracy on the frontier that other phases of life in America no longer provided. Social distinctions went by the board; the only superiorities that mattered were superior strength, or courage, or ability with an ax, a six-gun or a horse. The necessity of self-preservation bred an aggressiveness that remains one of the traits of the Westerner to this day. When his self-reliant nature overcame the trials of the trail and the tests of frontier life the settler developed a boastful confidence in his way of living that made him critical of other regions and skeptical of other ways of doing things.

In the later Southwestern towns life was easygoing and boisterous.

To the Far West went the more restless and venturesome, those who wanted to forget the past and whose past was better forgotten, the gamblers and the grog-shop men.

The mining and cattle communities had perforce to establish their own law and order, and out of their protective associations grew the first legislative bodies in the territories. As long as the lure of free land was held before the pioneer, American institutions were still being shaped and modified by the vital influence of the frontier on the national life. What the pioneer thought and what he did are reflected in the pattern of the life we live in the United States today. The great trails to the West—the Oregon-California, the Mormon and the Santa Fe —the roads that carried the main streams of immigration and trade, are today paralleled by concrete highways and steel rails, but the wagon ruts that ended in California and Mexico left a mark on the nation, its people and its history that neither the passing of time nor the hand of man can erase.

PART II The Santa Fe Trail

CHAPTER THREE

THE TRAIL-BREAKERS

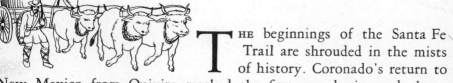

THE beginnings of the Santa Fe Trail are shrouded in the mists of history. Coronado's return to New Mexico from Quivira marked the first round-trip made by a white man between the Southwest and Kansas. But long years were to elapse before the trail was to see another. In the seventeenth century it was doubtless traveled by traders and an occasional missionary. In the next 100 years the Spaniards used it in desultory fashion; there was no particular reason why they should go to the Arkansas; there was every reason why they should keep out of the Indians' territory. But the French, on the other hand, found New Mexico a profitable market. Traders from the Illinois country dropped down the trail trod by Coronado's men and kept turning up in Santa Fe with considerable regularity, if in negligible numbers. Long after the treaty that extinguished France's American possessions, French trappers roved the territory west of the Mississippi, and New Mexico soon made it plain that they were not wanted. If any trade was to be done with the Indians, the Spaniards said, in effect, they would do it. They made an effort to establish trade routes from New Orleans and St. Louis; Pedro Vial headed an expedition from Natchez to Santa Fe and in 1793 led another party from Santa Fe to St. Louis.

But Santa Fe still slumbered on in incredible remoteness, connected with the world only by the busy road that led south to Mexico. Over the Chihuahua trail came caravans of Mexican traders to annual fairs in New Mexico. The Yankee traders had not yet made their way over the old trail from the north.

The Americans who did visit the capital did so under compulsion —they were captured by the Spanish and taken there willy-nilly, and their experiences in the jails of Santa Fe and the *calabozos* of Chihuahua were not of a nature to encourage others to explore Spanish territory. But the effort to open up trade with Santa Fe was soon to be made, despite the evident unfriendliness of the Spaniards and the hazards of the journey.

The year after the Louisiana Purchase, 1804, saw a Kaskaskia merchant named William Morrison dispatch Baptiste La Lande, a French Creole, from what is now Illinois to Santa Fe with a stock of goods. La Lande reached the capital successfully enough, but of his adventures on the way he unfortunately left no record. What he did leave behind was a bad reputation, for Morrison never saw him nor his goods again. Baptiste found, as Morrison had no doubt told him he would, that his goods sold high in Santa Fe. He found, too, that Santa Fe was a pleasant place and that the women were kind. He had made a discovery that later arrivals were to confirm—Santa Fe was a pleasure land of exotic delights and Latin graces, where the girls danced, smoked cigarettes and drank the wines of the province, and a new freedom pervaded the social customs. Baptiste decided to stay. He sold Morrison's consignment and kept the proceeds. He did well in his adopted country; when he died fifteen or twenty years later he left a large family and considerable property.

La Lande was followed to Santa Fe, somewhat inadvertently, by James Purcell, or Pursley as he is called in Pike's narrative. Purcell was a Kentuckian who had emigrated to St. Louis. The impulse that made him pack up and leave his home town apparently was not stilled with his arrival on the Missouri, for with two companions he set out on a trading venture to the plains. What their precise plans may have been underwent a sudden change when their horses were stolen by Indians and they were left to foot it across the prairie—not the best means of getting anywhere on the great plains. But they were lucky enough to fall in with another party going up the Missouri.

Purcell, after considerable wanderings in the wild and unexplored regions of the Platte, was soon trading with the Indians in the mountains of Colorado. Here he was asked by the Indians to go to Santa Fe to seek permission from the governor to allow them to remain in Spanish territory. In 1805 he set out with a company of Indians as guides and went down to the capital. Like La Lande, he stayed. The hospitality, customs and charms of the easy-going Spanish-Indian town won him, as they were to overcome many another visitor. And the day was drawing near when visitors would come down the trail in numbers that even the hospitable and welcoming people of Santa Fe could hardly have expected. For Pike, the explorer whose journal

62

stirred the American traders into bustling activity, was now on his way to the Southwest.

Only twenty-seven when he set out up the Missouri from St. Louis in 1806, Pike was hardly old enough to have taken a major part in the Wilkinson-Burr conspiracy; he was young enough, perhaps, to be used by the Commander-in-Chief for his own dubious ends. The role he played seems to have been that of innocent accomplice; General Wilkinson probably told him as much as he thought good for him and no more.

Pike visited the Pawnee settlements in Nebraska and Kansas. Turning southwestward, he reached the great bend of the Arkansas and thereafter followed the historic trail for a considerable distance. By November he had reached the Purgatoire River, but instead of veering southward toward the Spanish settlements he turned north to explore the mountains—in winter! At the end of January, 1807, after his party had suffered terrible hardships and had all but met with total disaster, Pike emerged from the ranges and struck the Rio Grande, where he built a fort.

In Pike's party was a surgeon, Dr. John Robinson, who had been commissioned by the irate Morrison back in Kaskaskia to catch up with Baptiste La Lande and try to collect the account for the goods that had disappeared down the Santa Fe Trail two years previously. Pike now dispatched Robinson to Santa Fe, ostensibly to present Morrison's compliments and bill to the rascally trader. In reality, Robinson was Pike's secret agent, sent to spy out the land and discover the strength of the Spaniards around the capital.

Pike had not long to wait before the results of the surgeon's visit to Santa Fe became evident. A troop of 100 Spaniards rode up to his stockade, prepared to take him back with them. Nothing could have suited the young commander better; Santa Fe was the place he had planned to reach, and in the company of the amiable Spaniard Don Fernandez he could now make the journey in comfort and safety. The trip south through New Mexico was an eye-opener to the American captives. At Ojo Caliente they saw the fandango for the first time, and all along the route they met with the courtesy and hospitality that had overwhelmed La Lande and Purcell. "In every place where we halted a moment there was a contest who should be our hosts," Pike wrote. At San Juan he met Baptiste La Lande, who confessed that he had been sent by the Spaniards to find out what Pike wanted and what he was really doing; it is highly probable that to them the young American appeared to be the advance party of a hostile army preparing to invade their territory. If they concluded as much they were not far off the mark.

In March the troop arrived at its destination. Santa Fe did not at first impress Pike. He remarked on "the miserable appearance of the houses." But the capital was to improve on further acquaintance. Governor Allencaster received the American civilly enough but took the precaution of relieving Pike of his papers, and before sending him further on his way to Chihuahua, where he was to be examined by the military commandant, Salcedo, entertained him at a "rather splendid" dinner.

Now Pike and his men began the journey south from Santa Fe, down the valley of the Rio Grande. Their escort proved sociable and diverting. As the cavalcade passed through the villages the men were entertained with music, dancing and wine. The Spanish commander would send a messenger ahead to the next town to warn the inhabitants of the approach of the American officers, instructing them to have their "handsomest young girls" on hand for a fandango. This pleasant captivity lasted the few weeks until Chihuahua was reached. Pike was received courteously by General Salcedo, who treated the Americans as honored guests—although he prudently retained their documents—and then had them escorted to the Texas border. Nearly a year after leaving St. Louis, Pike returned home.

His narrative opened new vistas of trade and adventure, the impelling motives that were to send men down the old trail by the thousands. In Santa Fe was a virgin market for the staples of Yankee commerce. Imported cloth sold for $20 a yard, linen for $4, iron was worth $1 a pound, tobacco cost $4 a pound. Of this rich trade the Americans had no part; all New Mexico's imported goods came from the Spaniards in Old Mexico. But the road to El Paso and Chihuahua was far longer than the trail to the Missouri; it was little wonder that Americans' eyes popped when they read Pike's journal.

But the Spaniards did not intend to give up their market to American interlopers without a struggle. The next expedition over the trail did not end so happily as Pike's. Three Missourians, James McLanahan, Reuben Smith and James Patterson made their way over the prairie in 1809 to obtain "geographical and commercial information," only to be intercepted on the Red River by a Spanish patrol. They were taken to Santa Fe and then led in irons to Chihuahua, and they spent the next two years in jail in Mexico. In the same year as they returned home, 1812, another party set out over the trail to meet a fate worse than had befallen McLanahan. Robert McKnight, James Baird and Samuel Chambers followed Pike's directions on the route to Santa Fe. The party got there but they were thrown into the *calabozos* of Chihuahua as spies, their goods were confiscated, and the men languished in the Spanish jails for nine years.

64

But the call of the Santa Fe Trail was strong indeed. McKnight returned to Chihuahua, and Baird and Chambers became Santa Fe traders even after their privations and injustices. The names of other Americans crop up in the half-light of the trail's history. The few of them who followed Pike's directions had their troubles, either with the Pawnees en route or with the Spaniards at their destination. But the birth-pangs of the trail were almost over. It had struggled hard for life in the centuries that had elapsed since Coronado; two events were now to set the tide of humanity running full flood down its broad lanes, across its wide rivers and over its arid deserts and arduous mountain passes. In 1821 the Mexican revolutionaries under Iturbide took Mexico City, ending the power of Spain, and in the following year William Becknell took wagons for the first time over the trail that only men and horses had traversed. The two events were complementary—for the first time the New Mexican frontier was open to American trade, and in Becknell's wagons were the goods that the inhabitants of Santa Fe, freed from their oppressors, awaited with eagerness. From that moment the trail was filled with a pageant of life and movement that surged down from the new civilization to the old. The bars were down, and the Americans were to be kept out no longer.

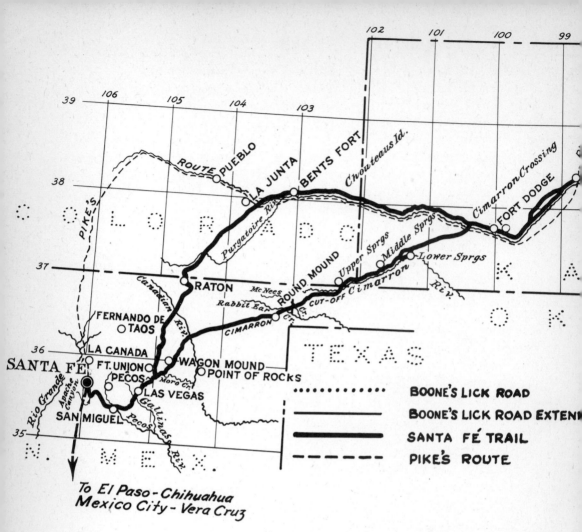

- - - - - - - - - - - - BOONE'S LICK ROAD

———————— BOONE'S LICK ROAD EXTEN[...]

═══════════ SANTA FÉ TRAIL

– – – – – – – – PIKE'S ROUTE

There were several starting points of the Santa Fe Trail—Franklin, Independence, Westport—but soon the threads came together into one strand. The Trail changed and expanded as it wandered across the prairie, but the landmarks and the camping grounds were etched unforgettably into men's minds. There never was a "road" as such— the Santa Fe Trail was not so much the ruts that disappeared over the horizon as the people who made them. There were few names on the land; there were only people on the march. From Council Grove, 145 miles west of Independence, the Trail struck off across Kansas past Diamond Springs to the ford of Cottonwood Creek. Here wagons had to be lowered by ropes down the stream's slippery sides and hauled up again by hand on the farther bank. The caravans now approached the Arkansas at Great Bend, where the short grass began. They followed the river to Pawnee Rock, where the travelers carved their names and began to think which route they would choose for the next stage of

66

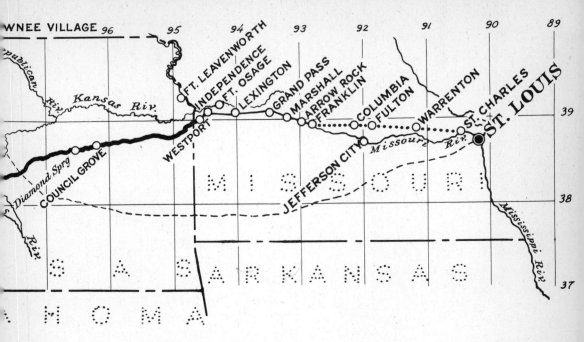

SANTA FE TRAIL

the journey to where Dodge City now stands. They could either follow the river or move inland a few miles and thus avoid the belts of sand through which it coursed. Farther up the river they had to decide once more whether to continue following the Arkansas and take the mountain route to Santa Fe that Pike had mapped, or whether, like Becknell, they would strike boldly southwest across the desert, across the Jornada del Muerto (Journey of the Dead)—that desolate, sun-baked stretch between the Arkansas and the Cimarron, where for more than fifty miles there was no water. Through the southwest corner of Kansas, into the tip of Oklahoma and into Colorado crawled the caravan, past Round Mound and Wagon Mound. If the travelers elected to follow Pike's footsteps they continued up the Arkansas to the fort built by the traders Bent and St. Vrain. From Bent's Fort they turned southward until they crossed the mountains over Raton Pass. Here they were doing well if they got their wagons over the huge rocks at the rate of a mile a day. Thereafter they crept along the foothills to Las Vegas where the two main trails joined, and continued westward to Santa Fe. En route they moved from the lush prairie to the short-grass region and finally to the desert; mirages shimmered before them, but it was the magic of Santa Fe that kept them moving over the 800 miles.

When Becknell's rawhide packages of Mexican silver dollars were dumped on the sidewalk and the money spilled out on the Missouri street, a new era opened. Thereafter Independence (above), a few miles below the future Kansas City, was no place for the faint-hearted. It was soon to become the busiest town in the United States west of St. Louis. By 1830 it had a blacksmith shop and supply stores, and the caravans to Santa Fe left regularly in the spring to return in the fall. Here the pack horses began the 800-mile trip laden with cottons, woolens, silks, velvets, cutlery and hardware. Each man took with him 50 pounds of flour, 50 pounds of bacon, 10 pounds of coffee, 20 pounds of sugar and enough salt for his needs. Later were to come the wagons with their teams of mules and oxen; later still the emigrants for Oregon and California thronged the town. In the thirties and forties a trip to Santa Fe was popular with adventurous youths. Those who could afford it went as proprietors, others found employment with the trains.

In those days Independence echoed to the shouts of the traders, trappers, mountain men, gamblers and merchants. The riotous frontier community busied itself in buying, selling, outfitting and revelling. "The wild and dissipated mountaineers," observed a contemporary writer, "get rid of their last dollars in furious orgies, treating all comers to galore of drink, and pledging each other in horns of potent whisky." The drivers and packers of the returning caravans shot their guns to give due notice of their approach and to assure a proper welcome. When they had unloaded buffalo robes and furs they were free to get rid of their hard-earned wages, and they proceeded to do it without loss of time. Whisky circulated at a rate that alarmed newcomers to the frontier settlements, where every man carried a loaded gun in his pocket, and an enthusiastic celebrant could find himself broke by morning. But the Trail was there waiting for him, and he could turn immediately to the solace of its remote silences and the romance to be found at its destination.

The Trail left the lush hardwoods of the Missouri country behind it as it struck off across the plain toward the buffalo grass. In this modern photograph the old riverbed can be seen.

Today, almost 100 years after their passing, the ruts still furrow the ground where the caravans jogged slowly across Kansas, along the Arkansas River, into the southeast corner of Colorado and over

Monuments throughout the West commemorate the settlers who went down the sunset trails. *The Pioneer Mother* stands in Kansas City's Penn Valley Park. The group is a typical example of such memorials.

the Raton Pass in the Rockies; or by the terrible desert cut-off from the Arkansas to the Cimarron River, through the northwest corner of Oklahoma, and thus down into New Mexico.

The early traders carried their goods to Santa Fe on muleback. Each mule in a pack train carried from 200 to 250 pounds at a cost of $12 per 100 pounds. They made an average daily trip of 15 miles, taking six or eight weeks on the journey. There were many dangers, the

most frightening being the ever-present possibility of attack by Indians.
The traders found need for all they could muster of courage and constant alertness, of diplomacy in meeting the redmen, backed by a
careful guard against treachery.

The white man was not always the innocent bystander. Often enough
he was the aggressor, and his treatment of the Indian was as savage
as he had come to expect at the hands of the tribesmen. While the
worst of the Indian fighting took place in the north and later with
the Apaches in Arizona, some trouble took place in the territory crossed
by the Santa Fe Trail. In consequence the Trail acquired a darker tinge
of danger; to the adventurous-minded its attractions increased. The
elemental hazards of nature were ever present; the dangers of hunger
and thirst, storms and floods were calculated risks that the traders
allowed for. But the greatest risk they ran was attack by the Indians.
The Arapahoes, Comanches and Pawnees were unholy terrors on the
Trail. They saw their hunting lands invaded and the buffalo herds on
which they depended for their livelihood being dispersed and exterminated. They had but to camp on the Trail and sooner or later a caravan
would come into sight. Woe betide any that lost their way or foundered
in the desert! The fatalities on the Trail were not many, but they
were ruthless and violent.

74

It was the violence of the attack that was remembered—the scalpings and the mutilations, the hapless survivors left to fend for themselves in the trackless desert after their wagons had been plundered and their livestock run off. The tales that were carried back to the Missouri settlements of these sudden affrays sharpened the old-timers' hatred of the Indian and heightened the newcomers' sense of adventure. The Trail was never a place for the careless and the unwary. Many a seasoned frontiersman met his death in an Indian ambush when he stooped to drink from a water-hole or wandered too far from the wagons in search of game. But even without Indians the Trail would have been dangerous enough. The oxen might take fright on the slightest provocation—at the jingle of their yoke-chains, at their own shadows on the ground. In an instant the herd would stampede in a thunderous rush.

Back in the frontier settlements Indian attacks on pioneers like the above were growing fewer as the population increased and as the redman was driven farther afield by the encroachments of civilization.

When Becknell proved in 1822 that wagons could be taken down the Trail intact he started a trek that lasted nearly half a century. Lone traders and wealthy proprietors followed his example.

Loaded wagons on the Santa Fe Trail weighed from 3,000 to 7,000 pounds. They were drawn by ten or twelve mules, or by six yoke of oxen, which latterly found greater favor with the freighters. At least an equal number of spare animals had to be driven with the caravan to replace those that wore out and fell by the way. The wagons were of the strongest possible construction to withstand the rigors of the trail; brightly painted when they left, they returned bleached, warped and shrunken, with their spokes and iron-shod rims bound with rawhide to keep them from falling apart. Among the heavy freight wagons

covered with Osnaburg sheeting there occasionally appeared the elegant
carriage of an invalid, making the trip to regain his health. Josiah
Gregg, the early chronicler of the Trail, began his journey thus in
1831; at the week's end he had taken to his pony and by the time the
buffalo range was reached he was "as eager for the chase as the sturdi-
est of my companions." Men were beginning to learn the joys of Western
life. Gregg spent the next nine years on the prairies. He became a
successful trader and wrote enthusiastically of the Trail, its dangers
and its allure.

In the early days of the Trail immense herds of buffalo ranged the prairie. They were the main food supply of Indian and traveler alike. The Santa Fe traders came upon them by the thousands, and their tracks cut innumerable lines across the empty plains. In the wake of the herds lurked the wandering Indian tribes, hunting them incessantly. The white man was soon to join the pursuit with equal ferocity. With his rifle he took a toll that made the Indians desperate. The New Mexicans drove out regularly into the plains to slaughter enough buffalo for their meat supply. Like the Indians, they jerked the beef by cutting it into thin strips and hanging it in the sun to dry. The traders on the Trail soon learned to hang the strips of meat on ropes strung along the sides of their wagons and leave them there to cure as they marched. The herds provided them not only with food but with fuel as well, for in the desert and on the plains where wood was lacking buffalo chips were gathered for the campfire.

In the 1820's the herds numbered millions. Through the thirties they were plentiful enough, but by the forties the decline was noticeable. The buffalo was easy to shoot, and hunters habitually killed more animals than they could use for food. Approaching a herd, the rifle-man could pick off several bulls before the rest would cease grazing around the fallen beasts and move off. The noise of a buffalo herd wallowing in a river could be heard for miles like the sound of rapids. A huge congregation of them would foul the stream for hundreds of miles, and a parched company of traders, their tongues hanging out between their blackened lips, would arrive at the water's edge only to find the longed-for draught bitter and polluted. Long acquaintance with this "buffalo tea," as they called it, may have been one reason for their unrelenting pursuit of the animal. The first sight of buffalo on the Trail was enough to send the caravan into a fever of excitement. Every horseman made off after the herd and even the drivers and packers followed them on foot with rifles, shotguns and pistols; the Mexicans snatched up their spears and bows and arrows. The hunt was soon over, and presently the aroma of broiling meat filled the air. Some hardened old-timers of the prairie did not wait for the steaks to cook—they ate the hot liver raw and seasoned it with gall. The tongue was a much-prized delicacy and the hump ribs made an unsurpassed soup. Without buffalo the way would have been much harder.

On the prairie the early travelers met storms like none they had ever known at home. The wind could blow with a force that overturned wagons. Tremendous thunderclaps sent the livestock into terrified stampede. It took hours to round them up and get under way again.

82

Hailstones larger than hens' eggs were not uncommon, and the rain covered the plains inches deep. Along the Arkansas rain might make the going heavy and delay the caravan; in the Cimarron desert it might be welcomed by men who had gone for days without water.

Each caravan appointed a captain who directed the travel during the day and designated the camping grounds at night. On the march the caravan first traveled in single file, often as much as a mile long. This left the wagons vulnerable to attack and resulted in loss of property and oxen, so the line was broken into four sections traveling abreast. This enabled them to form a hollow square in short order when trouble threatened and at night when they made camp. The livestock was driven inside the square, the campfires were lit outside, and the men slept around the circle in their buffalo robes and blankets, ready for attack. Around the fire they regaled each other with tales of distant Santa Fe, the charms of its dark-eyed damsels, the fandangoes they would attend and the Spanish wines and brandy that awaited them. Even the invalids slept in the open. The night dampness and dew of the East were absent, and the dry air of the high plains was found to be beneficial. Tents were rare, and only in rainstorms did the travelers take to the wagons for shelter.

84

Next in importance to the captain was the commander of the guard.
Every man in the party had to stand guard duty; none could evade it,
whether he were tourist or proprietor, except the invalid. The "common
law of the prairie" was adamant in demanding that everyone take his
turn. The sentinel stood his watch for one quarter of every second
night, listening intently for any sound that might betray a war party,
and crouching to scan the horizon for the outline of a hostile form.
Constant vigilance was indeed imperative to protect the caravan from
Indian attack and to prevent the livestock stampeding. Nearly every
caravan that traversed the Trail had a brush with the Indians. Shots
were exchanged, but the toll of human life was small in proportion
to the numbers of men engaged in the trade. No more than ten lives
were lost in the decade following Becknell's journey, but they were
lost in terrible circumstances that lingered long in the memories of
the white men—the Indian throng whirling down out of nowhere,
the scalpings and mutilations, the survivors left to die.

85

Indian attacks on the caravans, such as shown here, caused a storm of protest, resulted in demands for troops to protect them.

In 1829 Major Bennett Riley with four companies of the Sixth Infantry was detailed to accompany the traders as far as the international boundary.

Three decades later, troops were still fighting Indians; Chivington's massacre of Cheyennes and Arapahoes at Sand Creek was the most ruthless.

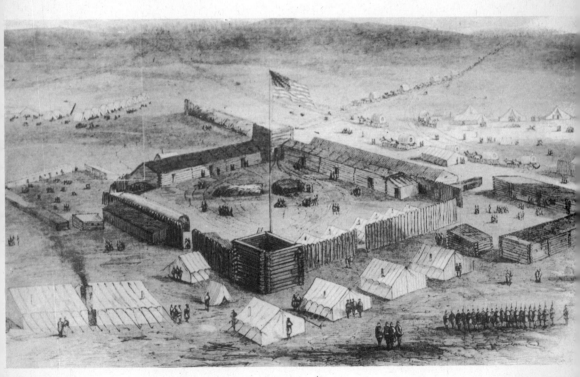

In the later days of the Trail, military supply forts like the above made the way easier for the traders and minimized the danger of attack.

At the end of the Trail lay Santa Fe, at the foot of the Sangre de Cristo mountains. It was not much to look at, with its low adobe huts and unpaved streets, but the spirits of the bullwhackers rose immeasurably as they topped the last rise and glimpsed the city they had come so far to see. The wagoners cleaned up, tied new crackers to their whips and fired their guns in delight. It was the moment they had slaved for over 800 miles of hardship. To the men from the Missouri settlements it was a new world, where Latin frankness combined with a natural gaiety to produce the appearance of license. All classes met at the faro tables; dice and cock-fighting were equally popular. The women in their silks and satins, their embroidered shawls, their short skirts without bustles and their low-necked chemises seemed immodest yet charming. They rolled cigarettes expertly and painted their cheeks with flour paste and vermilion. There was an incessant round of fandangoes and more formal balls. Little wonder that Santa Fe went to the head and lured men back time and again.

It was a city of illusions, glamorous only because it was part of another civilization. In the twilight of the Trail it dreamed on in remote seclusion, yet the two civilizations had been brought together and soon they were to become one. The Trail that had been the route of commerce became the path of empire. Troops marching to New Mexico past the lonely graves of those who had blazed the trail beat out a broader road than the oxen had trod, and the supply caravans rolling behind the Army of the West across the land made Santa Fe but a stop on the road to California. The Trail languished in the gold-rush days, eclipsed by the greater events that passed it by. It missed too the great migration to Oregon and California, yet it had made possible the opening of the Western lands. Freight and passenger services were in operation and railroads were inevitable. The Trail could not hold its own against the steel road. Yet it was the first of the great roads and for twenty years it was the most traveled. It had crossed the brink of civilization.

CHAPTER FOUR

THE RAILROAD COMES

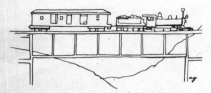

T HE dust clouds on the Santa Fe Trail were never thicker than in the 1860's. As the decade opened, more than 9,000 men, 6,000 mules, nearly 28,000 oxen and more than 3,000 wagons traversed the Trail. By 1866 these outfits had almost doubled, and between 5,000 and 6,000 wagons were sweeping the prairies. In another ten years the dust on the road to Santa Fe had begun to settle forever. The railroad had arrived.

There was every reason why the Atchison, Topeka and Santa Fe should have been built. The commerce over the Trail alone was enough to stir men's minds to the rich possibilities of rail transportation. But the roots of the Santa Fe lay much deeper than that. They were intertwined with the gold rush to California and Colorado; with Kansas' struggle for statehood; with the American rivalry with Mexico; with the nationwide clamor for a transcontinental railroad; with the subjugation of the Indians, and perhaps above all with the yearnings of the Kansas settlers for the development of their resources and the realization of their dreams.

Settlers were streaming into Kansas. From 1855 to 1861 the population increased from 8,600 to 143,000. This migration intensified the need for railroads at home, for the settlers were farmers who needed access to markets. The cattle drives from Texas gave encouragement to the enthusiasts who were planning railways in the West. In the East, New York and Chicago had been linked by 1849, and by 1860 relatively dependable service had been established. The effect on the economy of the country east of the Mississippi was enormous. Westerners watched its development with impatience and began to act on their own initiative. By 1857 the Kansas legislature had incorporated fifteen railroads, each the pet project of ambitious new towns.

91

Atchison, Leavenworth, Lawrence, Topeka, Kansas City and St. Joseph all had their own schemes; their projected roads ran in every direction. But the lure of Santa Fe was strong, for more than a dozen of them had the ancient city in the Sangre de Cristo foothills as their destination.

There were many impediments to the financing, construction and operation of Western lines. In the East the roads were built in settled territories where the prospects of future development and profits were evident. They were built, moreover, in the area where capital was most readily available. But the Western lines were projected in sections that many believed to be uninhabitable, despite the emigration to Kansas. To Easterners the proposed locale for new railroads was a desert where Indian tribes harried all who attempted to cross. Beyond lay the mountains, inhabited only by wild trappers and traders, which railroads would be unable to penetrate. Even the expansionist Senator Thomas Hart Benton, an enthusiast in the West, described the territory between El Paso and California as so bleak that "a wolf could not make his living." But then he was a proponent of a central route to the Pacific, and he had allowed partisanship to lead him into an overstatement that he probably did not believe.

But the men who put their faith in the West felt that all that was necessary was railroads to conquer the great distances. They had proved for themselves that the land that supported millions upon millions of buffalo was capable of growing tremendous crops; after the railroads, they believed, would come people, industry and commerce. And they were right. The railroads became powerful pioneers in the West. They paved the way for the sodbusters and then took their produce to the markets. The Atchison, Topeka and Santa Fe, the second great transcontinental link, pioneered the Southwest quadrant of the nation. From Eastern Kansas it stretched fingers southwest to historic Santa Fe. There were no towns along the route. Only Indians and buffalo contested the right of way. Towns were organized as the steel rails crept across the plains, settlers were brought in from abroad and the population multiplied into the millions. The line that was said to "start nowhere and go nowhere" eventually reached the Pacific, the Gulf of Mexico and Lake Michigan.

The Santa Fe was built on the assumption that the Great American Desert was a myth and that the West was capable of important agricultural and industrial development. Investment capital found little to attract it to Kansas, so early construction was begun on a shoestring. Financing was a long-delayed and disappointing process, and the line's operations were hampered by lack of working capital. Yet the men who built the Santa Fe stretched every dollar to the utmost and they

92

Topeka in 1870, two years after construction of the Santa Fe road began.

laid down the finest road that their limited resources and engineering techniques permitted.

Convinced that Kansas and the Western territories were high in soil fertility, rich in minerals and possessed of a moderate climate, they rightly concluded that transportation would bring the people necessary to make a prosperous economy. They knew also that the fortunes of the Santa Fe were inseparably linked with the economic development of the area. Therefore they went after the people; thousands of settlers were brought to the territory from as far away as Russia. Towns were laid out boldly along the advancing steel. True, some of them died; but those that lived were predestined to become the great cities of the plains.

With the coming of the railroad the old Santa Fe Trail fell into disuse. The new road was to handle infinitely more trade than could lumber painfully over the ox-bow trail. All the commerce that had been carried to Santa Fe in a year could now be hauled in one freight train, and delivery could be made in the old capital before the wagons could have advanced a few score miles out of Independence. Thus incredibly had time and space shrunk.

Topeka, the starting point of the railroad to the Southwest, was founded in 1854 on the banks of the Kaw and close to the great trails. By 1859 it was a bustling town of 1,200 citizens. Kansas was clamoring for a railroad of its own. Cyrus K. Holliday, one of the incorporators of Topeka, its first mayor and a member of the territorial legislature, wrote a charter for the Atchison and Topeka Railroad Company in 1859.

93

Cyrus K. Holliday, who planned the railroad to Santa Fe.

He was a man of unerring insight and imagination; all that came to pass in the development of the West he foresaw and predicted. But even his enthusiasm was not enough to overcome the prejudice against investing capital in Western railroads, and nine years were to pass before the railroad got under way. But in 1863 there was encouragement for the company's directors when the federal government turned over to the State of Kansas the odd-numbered sections of land for ten miles on either side of the projected railroad. In turn Kansas was empowered to grant the land to the road if it built to the Kansas-

94

Colorado state line by March 1, 1873. This land grant of nearly three million acres helped the young company's organizational difficulties, but it is interesting to note that the government doubled the price of the land remaining to it, so that it gave nothing of monetary value away, and that the conditions imposed on the railroad by its acceptance of the award proved a heavy burden on it. The rate discounts given to Uncle Sam have long surpassed the amounts realized from the sale of the land, and the concessions that were made on government shipments, until the Land Grant Act was repealed in 1946, swung the balance of this old transaction heavily against the company. At the moment, however, the grant was sufficient to renew the directors' pristine enthusiasm in their road and to cause them to change the name of the line, which did not yet go anywhere, to the Atchison, Topeka and Santa Fe Rail Road. But more significant than the land grant was an option, made in 1868, to buy a great tract of the Pottawatomie Indian Reservation in Eastern Kansas for $1 an acre for resale to provide construction funds and as collateral for loans. In the same year construction began at Topeka.

The new railroad headed neither for Atchison nor Santa Fe but toward the Kaw River, a few hundred yards from its starting point. To build the road a connection had first to be made with the Kansas Pacific, on the other side of the river and a bridge had to be built. Lumber came in over the K.P. line and was hauled by ox teams to the bridge site. Building went on through that winter and by the end of March, 1869, the span was completed. From the Ohio and Mississippi road the Santa Fe bought a locomotive, had it hauled to the end of their track by the K.P., named it the "C. K. Holliday" and lettered it "No. 1." This small locomotive made the first run over the road. The company was now ready to go ahead with its track-laying. It bought a day coach from the Indianapolis and Cincinnati Railroad, a dozen flat cars in Dayton, Ohio, and a handcar in Chicago. The line's first celebration came when the track stretched seven miles out of town toward Wakarusa Grove, and announced that a picnic was in order. It took thirty minutes to reach the end of track, but at that the picnickers made the trip faster than they had ever traveled to the grove before. The speed was reported to have approached fifteen miles an hour.

In a few weeks more the track reached Carbondale, where coal mines provided some freight revenue and supplied fuel for the locomotives. By September the line touched Burlingame, 26 miles from Topeka, and here the railroad met the old Santa Fe Trail. As the steel crept across Kansas a boom in land values preceded it. In Emporia lots that had gone begging at $500 were snapped up at $1,000 as the railroad's arrival was awaited. By midsummer of 1870 the 62 miles between

Track-laying over the flat prairie offered only minor difficulties.

Topeka and Emporia had been bridged, and the Santa Fe continued across the plains.

It was common labor that built the railroad. Pick and shovel and brawn did the work, and the number of men required was large although the territory as yet did not present many difficulties. The land was relatively flat and there were few curves, cuts, fills or bridges. Miles of ties and rails were laid right on the prairie without preliminary grading. Track-laying had begun with 50-pound iron rail and construction was poor when compared with present-day methods. There was no ballast, the ties were untreated and the rails were light. Few station buildings were erected, for there were no towns in existence and few were planned at that time.

Newton was a good example of the land boom that moved across the prairie a few miles ahead of the oncoming steel. In April, 1871, two pioneers arrived at the site in a wagon, put up a shack and named the town Newton. Six weeks later, when the Santa Fe announced that it would build through the place, there were 2,000 settlers there; when the grading gangs arrived Newton had a population of 6,000, most of them to be found in the twenty gambling tents that lined the main street. It was in this wild cow town that the Santa Fe was obliged to pause and take stock. The line was 134 miles out of Topeka and to earn the land grant it had to be at the Colorado border by March, 1873. It was estimated that the extension would cost some $5,000,000, and although the line was now making money this appeared more than the directors thought they could raise. Besides, no one was quite sure exactly where the Kansas-Colorado state line was, so in Newton the railroad stopped for a time.

Meanwhile T. J. Peter, who had built the first mileage of the Santa Fe, built the branch from Newton south to Wichita to intercept the herds moving north. He had the idea that the nesters would in time string their barbed wire far enough west to cut the trail herds off from the main line at Newton, and he offered the suggestion to the directors. They turned it down, probably because they were more concerned with getting the line west toward Colorado. Tom Peter thereupon rounded up a few friends and built the Wichita branch himself. The Santa Fe directors later saw the wisdom of his plan and leased the branch from his associates for thirty-five per cent of its gross earnings.

It was now May, 1872, and only ten months remained until the line must reach Colorado. Enough money to go on with construction had been found and J. D. Criley, who had built much of the Kansas Pacific line to Denver, was now given the task of pushing the Santa Fe track toward the state line. Criley managed to put down a mile of track a day, except on Mondays, when the effects of Sunday's exercises (not entirely devotional) cut the gang's progress to half a mile. Even more drastic was the aftermath of payday—only 500 yards of steel went down the next day. But the line kept moving across the prairie; it reached Hutchinson in June, Great Bend in July, Larned in August, Dodge City in September.

By Thanksgiving Day the construction gangs had put down some 300 miles in 230 days. Two days before Christmas the track arrived at what the surveyor thought was the state line. Most of the men started home in a work train. It was not until they had left that a government surveyor appeared to tell Criley that the state line was still four miles to the west. There was nothing for it but to move the tents of State Line City westward to the new stake, recall the work train and set to grading and track-laying again. But by now the line had run out of ties, rails and fastenings. There was only one thing to do—tear up four miles of sidings back along the line and get them over the Colorado border before winter set in. On December 28th the Santa Fe road was five yards into Colorado. There were no more rails or ties, but the line had won its land grant.

It was in the same year that the line extended eastward to Atchison.

On Saturday nights the construction gang backtracked to the nearest town; some

The people of Atchison had been complaining for a long time that the railroad had been giving them the cold shoulder. The extension was finally built and the first train from Topeka to Atchison made the run in April, bringing some more passenger traffic to the road. But in the West business was not so flourishing. In 1873 the line west of Dodge was hardly worth running trains over; the track ran out at Granada and there was no money left for new construction. It was not until another two years had passed that the railroad again headed west for Las Animas and Pueblo. There were incentives to building into Colorado: There were coal deposits in the vicinity of Trinidad and Canon City; timber on the Colorado mountain slopes promised lumber traffic to treeless Kansas as well as building materials and ties for the road, and mining operations in Southern Colorado needed transportation for their ores, machinery and supplies. Already Colorado was becoming a vacationists' mecca and was soon to be advertised as the "Switzerland of America." In the light of these factors the decision to build west was made. Las Animas was reached in September, 1875, La

98

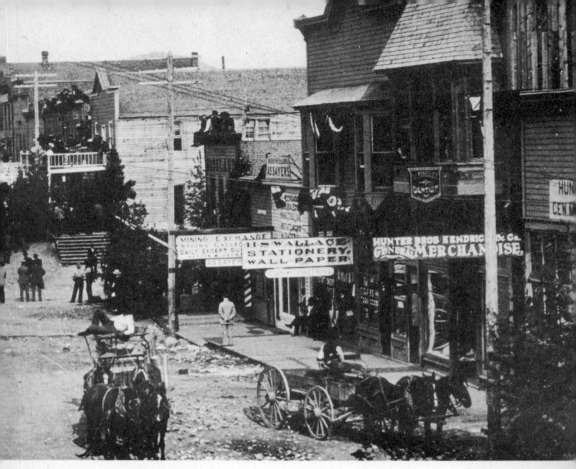

of these towns prospered and outlived the railroad boom.

Junta in December and Pueblo in February, 1876. The Pueblo *Chieftain*
jubilantly announced: "The biggest drunk of the present century will
occur here on the 7th of March."

In 1877 W. B. Strong became general manager of the road and with
Chief Engineer A. A. Robinson he projected the road down through
the mountains into New Mexico. To the west the way was barred by
the main range of the Rockies; to the south the way to Santa Fe was
barred by the Sangre de Cristo range. Barring the way of the Santa
Fe were also General William J. Palmer of the Denver and Rio Grande
railroad, which ran from Denver to Pueblo, and Collis P. Huntington
and his Southern Pacific. Palmer hoped to extend his D. & R. G. north
to intersect the Northern Pacific and the Great Northern, and south to
El Paso to make connection with the Mexican Central into Mexico
City. Both the Santa Fe and the D. & R. G. were in Pueblo, the former
from the east, the latter from the north. There was only one way west—
through the canyon of the Arkansas; there was only one way south
—over the Raton Pass where the traders had struggled to heave their

wagons over this major barrier in the early days of the Trail and where Richens Wootton, a trader and sheepman, had now built a toll road. He had graded some twenty-seven miles of highway from Trinidad on the north side to the Red River on the south, erected a hotel on the north slope and collected tribute from all comers over the pass except Indians; and there was only one way north to Denver—along the foothills of the Rockies, and the D. & R. G. was already there with a paying line. But the Santa Fe was determined to go somewhere. It was determined to get to Santa Fe for one thing, and beyond the Rockies lay the Pacific coast. In 1878 the line appropriated $20,000 for surveys from La Junta. Strong immediately sent his locating engineers to Raton Pass where the old trail over the mountains writhed its way up to nearly 8,000 feet. The Denver and Rio Grande, getting wind of the Santa Fe's plans, organized a grading crew and held it at Pueblo ready to grab the pass.

But the Santa Fe men moved too fast. When they heard that the D. & R. G. crew was to arrive in the morning they started out up the pass from Uncle Dick Wootton's tollhouse and hotel in the early hours. By 4 A. M. they were sufficiently far up to start grading and to warn the survey party above them to start shoveling up a rough grade. In the dawn's light they could see the rival grading crew toiling up the pass, too late. The Santa Fe had won Raton Pass by right of prior construction. By September the line reached Trinidad and approaches were blasted for a tunnel through the mountains. The track reached the Colorado-New Mexico line, north of the tunnel, in November, 1878; it was obvious that months would elapse before the tunnel was bored through, and it was decided to go over the top to the south side where another heading could be opened. The Raton switchback, 8,000 feet high, with six per cent grades and sixteen-degree curves, carried material over the summit and down to Willow Springs, which was soon to change its name to Raton. At the end of the year the last spike went in and the first locomotive to enter New Mexico breezed down the grade. Men and material could now be carried to the south portal of the tunnel, and in July, 1879, the two headings met and after completion of the tunnel the temporary switchback was abandoned. While it had been in operation, however, it had proved too tough for Santa Fe engines, and the line had the Baldwin Locomotive Works build the most powerful engine on earth. It was named the "Uncle Dick," for the man who owned the toll road through the pass, and numbered 204. Later this locomotive hauled the passenger train from Trinidad to Las Vegas and in 1880 handled the de luxe express from La Junta to Santa Fe.

North and west of Pueblo and across the Rockies, meanwhile, there had been silver strikes in the Leadville country in the fall of 1877. The

This 1878 locomotive was later remodeled (below), served until 1921.

new settlements were badly in need of transportation to take their ore out and to bring supplies in. There was only one pass through the mountains. It was the canyon of the Arkansas, the Royal Gorge. The Denver and Rio Grande road had surveyed the route but had filed no plats or profiles, and the Santa Fe once more attempted to seize a route by right of construction. One of the greatest of railroad wars was brewing. In April, 1878, the Santa Fe announced that it would build through the gorge into the new mining territory. General Palmer countered immediately by ordering his engineers to rush a crew to the end of track east of Canon City and proceed through the gorge. When the Santa Fe locator, W. R. Morley, arrived at Canon City, a D. & R. G. work train was coming up from Pueblo with a grading crew. He organized a working party outfitted with shovels from the local hardware store. When the D. & R. G. crew arrived the Santa Fe graders were already at work. Both sides started building rock forts at spots overlooking strategic points in the gorge to protect the workers, and simultaneously the battle of the courts began. Injunctions and writs were handed down daily while the two gangs fought it out in the gorge. Rocks were rolled down from the heights, bridges were burned, camps were raided, tools were thrown into the Arkansas, new grade was blasted with black powder or covered with rocks dynamited from above. The two roads began to wage war to lure men from each other. A Santa Fe special train rolled into Pueblo carrying 100 badmen under the fearsome Bat Masterson, and this well-gunned army proceeded to the canyon to guard the surveyors.

The fight collapsed temporarily when the financiers, perhaps scared of the publicity their roads were receiving, arranged a lease of the Denver system to the Santa Fe. The truce was short-lived. The Santa Fe claimed that the lease included the grade to Leadville; the D. & R. G. insisted that it did not. The Santa Fe now had the use of track from Pueblo to Canon City and used it to rush men and materials to the gorge. Then the D. & R. G. men built a rock barrier and manned it with riflemen. So the bitter battle went on until March, 1880, when under the terms of settlement the D. & R. G. agreed to pay the Santa Fe $1,400,000 for all construction west of Canon City and the Santa Fe agreed to abandon for at least ten years its plans to build to Leadville or Denver.

The Santa Fe now moved south. It reached Las Vegas in July, 1879, and Santa Fe in February, 1880. There had been some disappointment when it had been found impracticable to take the main line through Santa Fe as there was not enough business left along the old trail to justify the expense. A branch line was run up to the old capital from Lamy. The line went on through Albuquerque, San Marcial and Rincon. Here it branched, the southern leg heading for El Paso and the western for Deming, N. M. At this point the Santa Fe and the Southern Pacific were connected, and the Santa Fe thus had access to the Pacific over the Southern route. In March, 1881, the first Santa Fe train left Kansas City for the Pacific coast, and in the same year the line ran down over the Texas border to El Paso.

The Santa Fe now made another attempt to get to the Coast over its own track. In 1866 the Atlantic and Pacific road had got a charter to build from Springfield, Missouri, through Albuquerque and along the 35th parallel to the Pacific. By 1880 it had built only a few miles of track. At the same time, the St. Louis and San Francisco road, which owned seven-eighths of A&P stock, was as far west as Wichita. The 'Frisco and the Santa Fe now took over the A&P and began to build west from Isleta, 12 miles south of Albuquerque. By September, 1881, the line reached Holbrook, and work was held up for six months while a bridge was thrown over the Canyon Diablo, 26 miles west of Winslow,

102

Arizona. This canyon took 15 months to span with an iron bridge said to be capable of carrying thirty times the weight of any train that could run over it. Parts of the bridge were freighted across the desert from railhead and assembled at the site. It cost more than $250,000; it was 560 feet long and was 225 feet above the canyon bed.

Westward the line went to Needles, where the Santa Fe bridged the Colorado River in August, 1883. There the railroad made connection with the Southern Pacific and was able to reach the coast over a much shorter Southern Pacific link. The Colorado bridge was washed out in the following year and until it was repaired freight, passengers, baggage and mail were ferried across to the Southern Pacific connection in flatboats. The Santa Fe was moving steadily toward the Pacific, but it was still 630 miles from San Francisco, 340 miles from Los Angeles and 435 miles from San Diego.

But construction eastward from San Diego had already been underway for nearly two years. In 1881 the Santa Fe had shipped rails from Antwerp round the Horn and more had come month by month. The first passenger train from San Diego to San Bernardino was run in September, 1883, despite the efforts of the Southern Pacific to hinder construction into San Bernardino and the Cajon Pass to join the main Santa Fe line. In 1884 the Santa Fe leased the Needles-Mojave line from the Southern Pacific with trackage rights into San Francisco and an agreement to buy the line for $30,000 a mile. The Santa Fe could now run 170 miles west of Needles to Barstow, then build 78 miles to San Bernardino, over the pass, and connect with its San Diego link.

The work was begun in 1885. The Cajon Pass traverses two mountain ranges—the San Bernardino and the San Gabriel. The last spike was driven in the pass in November and the line was opened in the middle of the month. The first through train left San Diego on November 16, 1885. The Santa Fe then bought the Los Angeles and San Gabriel road and built another track to connect San Bernardino with Los Angeles. Thus the railroad went into California at two coast terminals. The two rival roads—Southern Pacific and Santa Fe—now started a fierce rate war. The Santa Fe cut the price of the ticket between the coast and the Missouri to $10; the Southern Pacific cut it to $5. For one day at the climax of the fight the fare was $1. Naturally enough there was a land boom of fantastic proportions. Farmers in the Middle West sped out to California to see what the land looked like, took one look, and hastened home to sell their stock and bring out their families. New cities sprang up along the right of way; in 1887 between San Bernardino and Los Angeles 25 new cities appeared in 36 miles of track.

The Santa Fe had reached the Pacific. Now its eyes turned in the

103

This was Guthrie, Oklahoma, twenty-one days after the land "run."

other direction. The railway was operating under the disability of having the farmers in its territory ship their produce to Kansas City and then transfer to another road to get it into Chicago. The danger to the Santa Fe in this was that if any east-of-Missouri road built into Santa Fe territory it could offer through shipment to Chicago, and there were several roads that already had their sights set for operation in competition with the A. T. & S. F. The Santa Fe planned a straight-line route into Chicago and as a first move it acquired the Chicago and St. Louis road. In 1886 it opened construction offices in Kansas City and Chicago after surveying the road in secret. The undertaking was a gigantic one. In nine months 350 miles of new line were located, surveyed, graded and laid, 100 miles more were rebuilt and five big bridges were built across major rivers, not to mention scores of smaller ones. Construction started in March, 1887. The location crossed 13 other roads. Some 7,000 men were put to work. The bridges over the Mississippi, the Grand, the Missouri, the Illinois and the Des Moines were built at record speed. Nearly $7,700,000 were spent on real estate and construction in Chicago, and new de luxe equipment was bought. The new vestibuled trains started out for Kansas City in April, 1888.

At the same time the Santa Fe probed south to the Gulf of Mexico. Galveston business leaders had built the Gulf, Colorado and Santa Fe road—no connection with the A. T. & S. F.—to break the stranglehold exerted by Houston on Galveston's trade; they planned to go north to Fort Worth, missing Houston, then on to Santa Fe. They had begun construction in 1875 and had reached Fort Worth in 1881. Meanwhile the Santa Fe, building south, was headed for Texas. The Gulf line had no outlet to the north; it decided to sell to the Santa Fe. To connect with the Gulf the Santa Fe got a charter to cross Indian Territory south from Arkansas City. Grading and track-laying were begun in 1886, and in the following year through trains were operating between Galveston and Arkansas City and on to Kansas City.

The depression of 1887 cut deeply into revenue. W. B. Strong was accused of over-expansion and he resigned in 1889. Allen Manvel succeeded him, and came in facing huge losses for 1888 operations. He reorganized finances, cut costs and went after new tonnage and passengers. In 1890 he bought some 1,300 miles of the 'Frisco to get into St. Louis; it cost $22,511,687. In the West the Colorado Midland road was bought. In little more than 20 years the Santa Fe now owned or controlled track from Chicago to the Gulf of Mexico, the Pacific coast at San Diego and Los Angeles, and to Denver. Much new equipment and power had been acquired in 1887–89, but now a great part of this had to be stored, for the California boom had collapsed, passenger business had dwindled and freight rates were dropping.

In 1893 the panic was on. More than 600 Western and Southern banks crashed, J. W. Reinhart succeeded Manvel as president of the Santa Fe, and at the end of the year the line went into receivership. During the receivership a reorganization plan was worked out for the rehabilitation of the 9,344 miles of railroad with its capital of $102,000,000 and its debt load of $233,595,248. In December, 1895, E. P. Ripley became president. The system was sold to the reorganization committee, who turned over the assets to a new corporation— the Atchison, Topeka and Santa Fe *Railway*. Holliday was an incorporator of the new company, as he had been of the old, and served for a time as director. In 1897 the Santa Fe regrouped its lines by buying, selling and trading, which gave it through lines from Chicago to Denver, Los Angeles, San Diego, El Paso and Galveston.

Arizona, meanwhile, was still trying to get a railroad down into her copper country. Goods were still being freighted by wagon trains and Arizona's transportation down around Prescott and Phoenix was still in the horse and burro stage. Early railroad promoters had been either scared off or so badly hampered in their operations by the cattle men that the only railroad in the territory, the Prescott and Arizona Central, was barely limping along. The cattle men considered that railroads would break up their holdings and bring in miners to stake claims all over their grazing lands. Up to this point, therefore, railroading in the area had been more than usually hazardous. The Santa Fe entered the scene in 1892, when the first spike of the Santa Fe,

105

Through Cajon Pass, traversing the San Bernardino and San Gabriel ranges,

Prescott and Phoenix line was driven at Ash Fork, and the new road started south. Track got to Prescott the following year and reached Phoenix in 1895.

The road had still no outlet to San Francisco but that, too, was on the way. In 1895 San Francisco leaders planned a railroad from Stockton to Bakersfield to serve the little San Joaquin Valley towns that had been hard hit by excessive freight rates from San Francisco. They shipped the rails for the new road by sea from New York, and by 1898 the line had reached its southern terminus at Bakersfield. From Stockton track was laid over swamp and through mountain ranges to

106

a turn-of-the-century Santa Fe train passes the gateway to Los Angeles.

East Bay, across from San Francisco. The Santa Fe acquired the San Francisco and San Joaquin Valley Railway and began operating it in 1900. In July the first ferry left San Francisco for the Santa Fe terminal at Richmond—the first direct Santa Fe service from San Francisco to Chicago. In slightly more than forty years the Santa Fe had bridged half a continent and opened a new American empire. Few were the reporters—and fewer still the artists—who were on hand to record the hazards which had to be overcome. But the picture and print record of that achievement gives more than a hint of what was, undoubtedly, the most tempestuous period of railway expansion.

Railroads had come to the United States in 1827. By 1860 their economic benefits had been felt east of the Mississippi.

But in the West the stage coach was still the only means of public transportation; work on the first railway had not yet begun.

By 1875, however, thousands of men were laboring in cuts such as these.
The era of the bulldozer and power shovel was far in the future.

Where possible the road conducted its own lumbering operations.
There was no timber on the prairies, of course, and ties had to be

floated down the Arkansas and hauled up to railhead. But farther west the road was able to cut its own ties as it went.

With every man a walking arsenal and well fortified internally, gunplay was a daily occurrence. This movie still reproduces a typical scene.

Although shacktown restaurants and "chop houses" were plentiful, most of their stock-in-trade was liquid.

Many of the rail-end towns withered and died when the construction gangs moved ahead. False fronts came down and bars closed up.

Others continued to flourish long after the cattle-shipping business had fallen away. Settlers kept them alive and made them grow.

All of them thrived in their hey-day. Gambling and drinking were their
principal industries. Cowboys delighted in shooting up the cattle towns.

Cash-laden after their long weeks on the trail, they soon contrived to
separate themselves from their earnings at the faro and monte tables.

114

Saloons, dance halls and bawdy houses competed for railroaders' and cattlemen's trade. Occasionally an itinerant preacher held forth.

The early hotels and boarding houses, in keeping with the character of the frontier towns, were wildly competitive.

Justice in the new towns was swift and sure; it had to be if the better element hoped to keep the upper hand. Courts were few and far between, and informal in the extreme.

116

When the shootings became too frequent and things looked to be getting out of hand, the citizenry staged a "necktie party" to restore order, then relaxed until another hanging was necessary.

Railroad operations around Dodge City were hazardous. Cowboys delighted in shooting out the headlights. Hoboes rode the rods.

In addition to their other duties, conductors had to throw badmen off the trains; occasionally they themselves were bounced off by tramps.

Cowhands on the spree would hold up trains and divest passengers of their cash and valuables. But they were seldom killers.

The real killers were the professional train robbers. Organized robberies became popular in the deserts of New Mexico and Arizona when the railroads started expressing large sums of money and gold. It was standard practice to carry two Winchesters and 100 rounds of ammunition in the engine, and west of Dodge City there was a rack of Winchesters in the baggage car. Much shooting attended the holdup, and the best-laid plans of the bandits went awry in at least half of the attempts. But many railroad men lost their lives when the robbers shot without provocation.

A couple of the gang would hide on the train and climb over the tender. They would order the engineer to stop at a previously determined spot.

There the rest of the gang would be waiting to begin looting. They killed if need be, and when the job was done they rode off into the countryside. These pictures, and those on the three preceding pages, represent the Eastern concept of life on the frontier.

The buffalo wandered at will over the tracks, and frequently trains were blocked by immense herds. One engineer took hours to ease through a mass of animals that appeared to stretch to the horizon, packed so closely together that the track could not be cleared. The railroad took advantage of the opportunity to schedule hunting-trip

trains. "Sportsmen" shot buffalo from the windows and hunters slaughtered them ruthlessly. In 1873 the Santa Fe shipped more than 250,000 hides. The bones were collected for fertilizer. One hundred skeletons made a ton of bones and sold for $8; more than $2,500,000 worth were shipped east before the trade came to an end.

Storms and prairie fires were a serious threat. Many fires were started by sparks from the locomotive, and the company tried new smoke-stacks with complicated arresters of wire.

Snow plagued the line in winter. The company lacked funds to buy snow fences and the light locomotives were unable to cope with the drifts.

The Indians who roamed the Western half of Kansas did not take
kindly to the railroad idea. They rarely killed, but surveyors worked
under armed escort. The tribesmen occasionally burned the ties and
took pleasure in tearing down telegraph wires, delaying and menacing
trains.

This was the first Santa Fe train, built in 1868. It made a run of 17 miles

The road had fought Indians, weather, robbers and the plain cussedness of human nature before it reached Colorado. This passenger train was

from Topeka, Kansas, to Carbondale on its first trip.

buried in the snow for five days near Dodge City, a typical obstacle to the establishment of regular, dependable service.

The Santa Fe reached the Colorado border in 1873 within the stipulated time. In 1875 it stretched backward also to Kansas City, and in the next year it extended a spur to Pueblo and came in contact with the

Denver and Rio Grande for the Raton Pass where the wagons had struggled painfully through the mountains. On into Arizona went the steel rails, over the Canyon Diablo.

129

In 1905 a chartered train carrying Death Valley Scotty completed the

When the Valley Road, later to be acquired by the Santa Fe, reached Fresno in 1896, the citizens proudly celebrated the occasion as above.

trip from Los Angeles to Chicago in 44 hours, 54 minutes, a record.

The San Diego *Union* said editorially in 1885 that the coming of the Santa Fe might well "start a period of moderate expansion."

131

CHAPTER FIVE

UNTIL THE RAILROAD CAME, THE SANTA FE
TRAIL WAS A TRADERS' ROUTE; BUT WITH
THE RAILROAD CAME THE SETTLERS MOVING
TO PERMANENT HOMES IN THE REGION.

PEOPLING THE PRAIRIE

B Y 1873 the Santa Fe ran out from Topeka over the prairie as far as the Colorado state line, with branches to Wichita and El Dorado. But there were few people along the line and few tons to be carried. What the young railroad needed was some freight traffic. Without settlers there could be no business. But the Santa Fe did have one big asset—its land grant. By the terms of the federal award, building past the Colorado line within the stipulated time entitled the road to some 3,000,000 acres. It was to receive every odd-numbered section for ten miles on each side of the track. But in Eastern Kansas, which was now fairly well settled, this land was no longer available. The road therefore got "in lieu" lands farther west—half the lands on a strip forty miles wide from Emporia almost to Kinsley, and thence half of a twenty-mile strip as far as Colorado. The land grant resembled a checkerboard when plotted on a map, and in all entitled the Santa Fe to claim 6,400 acres for each mile of mainline track. Much of it was bottomland in the Arkansas River valley, and in normal years it would produce great crops. But the grant was unfenced, unmarked, unclaimed and unknown. At the time it was awarded the value of the land was negligible; until the railroad reached it, it had been worth little or nothing. What made it valuable now was that the railway could bring food and supplies to settlers and take their crops to market.

In 1874 the grasshoppers came to Kansas. There were times that year when the Santa Fe seemed near disaster. What farmers there were along the route almost starved. Gaunt and lean, they drove into the settlements looking for food. They began to sell their trinkets and their heirlooms. The Santa Fe brought back disheartened settlers without charge.

Panic scared Eastern investors from the railroads. There was no more money for new construction and precious little for maintenance of way. In the circumstance it looked like a hopeless task to sell land, but the Santa Fe had to try. It borrowed $1.25 an acre on certain lands and spent $3,500,000 rebuilding its trackage and establishing a new land department.

Agents were appointed in the new towns along the grant to push the sale of lands and co-operate with Eastern representatives. In the East ministers, teachers, lawyers and newspaper editors were commissioned to sell the people on Kansas. Tons of literature were distributed and land seekers were given special rates, usually half-fare; whatever was paid for tickets could be applied dollar for dollar on the initial installment for any land purchased. The agents traveled through the Eastern states, organizing parties and shepherding them out to the Santa Fe lands. Amish settlers had come from Pennsylvania about 1871 and developed two communities in Marion County. The settlements were about 23 miles apart, and in order to maintain communication between them the Amish ploughed a furrow all the way from one to the other to serve as a guide over the open prairie. These early Mennonites from the East were the forerunners of the thousands who were to come from Europe.

Literature about Kansas was widely circulated in Europe. Germans and Swedes began arriving. In 1874 Mennonites from Russia bought 100,000 acres and in the same year the great influx began. Their arrival in New York excited curiosity and interest. Soberly dressed in dark clothes, the men long-haired and bearded, they started off for Kansas. When they set foot in Topeka the people were inclined to jeer at their dress and their strange ways until they began flashing more money than Kansas had seen in many a year. Then nothing was too good for them. They were received at the State House by the Governor.

The fall of 1874 was a critical one in Kansas. Grasshoppers had consumed every vestige of green, crops were laid waste and hundreds of sodbusters had returned East. But neither blizzards, droughts nor grasshopper plagues daunted the incoming Mennonites. They bought the equipment of the beaten settlers who had made their motto "In God we trusted, in Kansas we busted," and they set to work preparing their lands and building houses.

The Santa Fe had more than the elements to contend with. Competition was tough from other railroads trying to lure the new settlers to Iowa, Nebraska and Missouri. But the Santa Fe cut its rates and its land prices, hauled building material free for a year, and chartered a liner to bring the Mennonites' agricultural equipment and household goods from Russia. The Kansas legislature, in an important move,

134

amended the military service law to read that members of a religious sect which forbade bearing arms might be exempt from service.

The Mennonites built their houses of sod or lumber in communities with the church and school in the center. The cattle towns did not appreciate settlers who broke the sod, ran fence lines and generally interfered with the untrammelled life of the prairie. But the Mennonites were hard-working farmers who were enormously successful with the land. More important, they brought their own grain with them from Russia and popularized the growing of hard red turkey wheat, which alone meant millions of dollars to the grain country.

In these drought years of 1874–75 the Santa Fe had to haul tremendous tonnages free to save its settlers. It hauled out thousands of bushels of seed grain free to farmers. In 1875 the crops came back with 80,000,000 bushels of corn and 13,000,000 bushels of wheat. Since that time in several single years Kansas has produced more wheat than all of Canada. At times it has produced more than one-fifth of the national supply. In 1877 and 1878 the Santa Fe started a new land rush to Kansas. By the end of the latter year it had sold 850,000 acres for around $4,000,000. It is doubtful if the railroad made much profit on the sale when the service it gave is taken into consideration. It had spent huge sums chartering steamers, running special trains, sending colonizing agents to Europe and Russia, cutting transportation rates on lumber, household goods and farm implements. But it established colonies of farmers who were later to build up a heavy freight business for the road. What the line set up was a permanent prosperous population along its route. It was these people who converted the barren prairie into farms and orchards. Commercial cities sprang from the plain, local manufacturing began, and consumer goods spread out in ever larger circles until the Southwest was a factor in the national economy.

Immigrants sometimes made scenes when they were met on shipboard by quarantine officials and forced to undergo vaccination.

From Germany, Sweden, Russia, Italy, they poured ashore at New York, Boston and Philadelphia, bound for the western lands.

Their dress was strange and they brought new customs with them, but these Persians were soon to be an integral part of America.

137

National groups like these Sicilians with their strange clothes and manners were soon to be swallowed up in the American West.

In the Far West the wagon trains of the settlers dotted the prairie. The newcomers were soon to add their number to the throngs.

The journey through Kansas was formidable, even by railroad. The top speed permitted passenger trains was but 20 miles an hour. The coaches were crowded, the seats were hard and uncomfortable and the train jounced and swayed over the light roadbed. Even so, it was a far better mode of travel than plodding behind a team of oxen or clinging to the seat of a teetering wagon.

Sleeping cars had not yet been introduced and passenger coaches had a seating capacity scarcely half of those used today.

Passengers brought their food with them. In summer flies infested the coaches and in winter heating was a difficult problem.

The operating difficulties faced by railroads of the era made schedules erratic; high winds, for example, could delay trains several hours. Among the hardships passengers suffered were long waits for late trains. Stations were ill adapted to accommodate the traveling public in comfort, and hotels and eating houses were for the most part non-existent.

In Colorado and Arizona some strange characters were turning up in the mining towns. The arrival of the dude at the diggings was the occasion for much ribald mirth on the part of old-timers.

Early settlements along the railroad were sometimes mere dugouts at first, until more substantial buildings could be erected. They were excellent shelters against the violent wind storms.

143

From cuts and fills such as this grew the rail-end shacktowns. The

Jerry-built homes, towns and stations sprang up as the road went westward. This was the first Santa Fe "depot" in Dodge City.

144

camp moved on five or ten miles at a time as the line progressed.

The early Kansas settlers built sodhouse homes. They did not prefer them to log cabins, but there was no lumber available.

145

Land was the all-consuming interest of the hour, land lotteries the greatest attraction. The settlement of Oklahoma raised the land fever to boiling point. The Santa Fe had crossed the Indian Territory before

the area was opened, and was prepared to meet the enormous demands for service. Boxcars were loaded with contestants' belongings and coaches were assembled at the borders.

When the gun was fired the trains steamed forward to compete with those on foot, on horseback and in wagons. Clerks and agents had gone ahead into Oklahoma in order to handle the business.

NOTICE
TO
IMMIGRANTS!!

As there are in our City a number of men with remarkable principles, who go among those who have newly arrived and offer to sell or lease to them the *Public Land* in and about this place, thus imposing upon the unsuspecting. The latter are hereby notified that the vacant land in Sacramento City and vicinity, is open for *ALL*, free of charge ; but, they can make either of the following gentlemen a present of a few thousand dollars, if they have it to spare. Such favors are eagerly sought and exultingly received by them. In fact, some of them are so solicitous in this matter, that, if they are not given *something*, they will *almost not like it*, and even threaten to *sue* people who will not contribute to their support. Those who have made themselves the most notorious, are

Barton Lee,	Prettyman, Barroll & Co.,	Warbass & Co.,
Burnett & Rogers,	A. M. Winn,	J. Sherwood,
Hardin Bigelow,	S. Brannan,	James Queen,
Pearson & Baker,	Hensley, Merrill & King,	Dr. W. G. Deal,
Thomas M'Dowell,	Conn. Mining and Trading Co.,	Eugene F. Gillespie,
R. J. Watson,	Paul, White & Co.,	T. L. Chapman,
J. S. Hambleton,	W. M. Carpenter,	Dewey & Smith,
Starr, Bensley & Co.,	R. Gelston,	E. L. Brown,
	John S. Fowler.	

Sacramento City, June 14, 1850.

"Sacramento Transcript" Print.

By order of the Settlers' Association.

But the best lots were gone long before the starting signal. "Sooners" had gone ahead to stake out their claims. Years before, in California, settlers had come up against a similar breed and had learned how to handle them. The poster above, revealing them to the public, was one effective way. All manner of men took part in the settling of the West, and the rogues were well represented.

Those who had patiently awaited the lawful process of occupying the land gave the sooners short shrift and ran them off their illegal claims. But often men who settled legally on lands where they were not wanted were harshly treated too. Cattlemen bitterly resented the intrusion of homesteaders onto the open range. They thought nothing of tear-

ing down the nesters new fences, burning their shacks, destroying their livestock and if need be killing the newcomers who proposed to farm the land they had been accustomed to use. Here a mining community turns equally ruthlessly on that varmint of the goldfields, the claim-jumper.

In the early days of railroad construction in Arizona the U. S. Cavalry escorted the stage coaches through the Apache country.

"Public relations" with the dispossessed Indians were, presumably, improved when the Guthrie Board of Trade invited Iowa redmen to visit the city.

But relations between the railroads themselves were as rugged as the men who built them. Bat Masterson, the famed Marshal of Dodge City, whose gunmen guarded the Santa Fe surveyors in the Royal Gorge, may have looked handsome in his bowler, but he appeared otherwise when battling the boys of the D. and R. G.

153

The gold rush to California a quarter-century before had spurred the

154

illustrators to some far-fetched conceptions of ocean and air travel.

Caustic and satirical cartoons filled newspapers and magazines.

lampooning the incongruities of the treasure-hunting hordes.

Similarly the coming of the railroads was reflected in the art of the period. Their social and political influences in welding diverse peoples, sections and customs into the homogeneity essential to unity were far-reaching and deeply pervaded the national life. The artists and lithographers of the time were quick to seize on the interest and excitement that railroads brought to the West, and their output was a valid contribution to the lore and literature not only of American railroading but of the development of the nation. The artistic content of their output need not be too closely examined; more interesting is their evident awareness that the railroads solved the Indian question, killed off the buffaloes, pioneered the land, supplanted the covered wagon and the stage coach, and symbolized the march of progress.

158

THE LIMITED MAIL

NELLIE SAVES THE LIMITED MAIL

ELMER E. VANCE'S FAMOUS RAILROAD PLAY

Elmer Vance's play, advertised in the poster shown above, was one of many that seized on the dramatic possibilities of the new era with its heart-stopping escapes and its heroines who flagged the train.

159

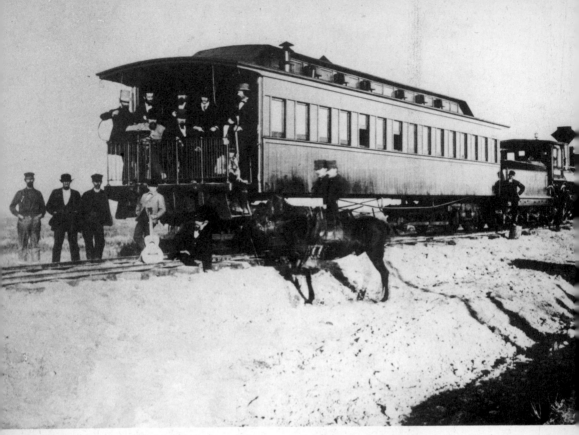

During the seventies and early eighties the men were paid on the job from the pay car. Once a month it raced over the line as an extra train, paying the construction crews in gold and silver. Later as the territory developed and banks were established along the line, checks were distributed through the road's agents, and the pay car was run only on occasions when large numbers of men were employed in a section of the country without bank facilities. It was not unusual to pay out from $60,000 to $90,000 in a day. Jim Moore, the paymaster, traveled considerable distances from one locality to another during the night so that the whereabouts of the pay car should not be well known. It was protected by one or two special officers, and there was no loss by robbery. The pay car contained an office and accommodations for two or more persons; officers of the railway frequently used the pay car to make inspection trips. The rear door of the car was divided so that the upper half could be opened like a window. The men crossed the rear platform and announced their names as they arrived at the wicket. The above picture was taken in Eastern Colorado at the rail-head in 1879. Jim Moore is astride the mule, for some unaccountable reason. He wears two heads here because snapshots were unknown then and the mule refused to stand still.

160

In July, 1885, Cyrus Holliday (top hat) attended the Brotherhood of Locomotive Firemen's picnic excursion to Fort Leavenworth. The first locomotives the Santa Fe used were the 4-4-0 type with a tractive power as low as 7,900 pounds. There was little change in type for the first twelve years, and they were years filled with difficulty. The water for the boilers was hard, the boilers scaled rapidly and the flues burned out every three months in Western Kansas. But while the immigrants were moving in, the road was kept busy hauling freight in both directions. The westward traffic consisted of lumber, hammers, plows, harness and the supplies and effects of the settlers. Tons moved East were cattle, sheep, hogs, coal, grain, buffalo meat, hides and bones.

In 1886 and 1887 a fleet of engines was bought from the Schenectady works. Some of the road's old locomotives gave sixty years of service. A few of these early engines had injectors, but most were fitted only with old-fashioned hand pumps. Good water had to be hauled long distances in these days, and two wooden tanks bolted to a flat car and equipped with a rubber hose served as water car. There were no telegraph facilities over long stretches of the prairie. The train crew had no caboose; they had to hole up in a boxcar, sitting on sacks of wheat or crates of supplies. Sometimes a cord was unwound from the last car to the engine bell; if the train broke in two the bell clanged, whereupon the crew roused themselves and clubbed the brakes. Some of the first trains over the mountains carried notices requesting passengers not to get off to pick flowers while the train was in motion.

The days of the stage coach were numbered now, although there were great tracts throughout the West where it remained the only means

of public conveyance long after the railroads had spanned the continent.
Here the movies recapture a symbolic moment.

When there was walking to be done in the desert . . .

Las Vegas became the Carlsbad of America. The famed Montezuma, a resort hotel, was built to accommodate wealthy world travelers.

. . . it could best be done by taking to the tracks.

Far up in the mountains silver strikes were made at Leadville and Cripple Creek. Soon dozens of mines were in production.

Meanwhile the towns tapped by the Santa Fe were growing apace. In the late eighties Kansas Avenue, Topeka, looked like this.

The depot at the same period was assuming the typical busy appearance of railroad stations many hundreds of miles to the east.

Far to the west, Trinidad, Colorado, looked like this. It was reached by the line in 1878 in its projection to New Mexico.

In Phoenix, Arizona, the court house stood in solitary splendor and local transportation was in the "Toonerville trolley" stage.

The dining car had not yet come into use in the West and the problem
of feeding the travelers who were now crossing the prairie in ever
greater numbers became acute. Schedules were slow, and the time
spent on journeys was three or four times as long as is required today.
There were no train "butchers" with milk and sandwiches, and travelers usually brought their own provisions whether eating stops were
made or not. The custom at the eating stops was to hold the train
some 20 minutes while passengers bolted whatever was to be had at
monopolistic prices—week-old coffee, salty ham and doubtful eggs.
The advent of Fred Harvey and his new restaurant system in 1876 put
an end to that. His first lunchroom at Topeka was spotless, the dishes
sparkled, the menu offered variety and the prices were moderate.

168

It was the first of the Harvey Houses that were to stretch from Chicago to California and Mexico. Managers and chefs were recruited from Europe and the East, and the chain was expanded to include sumptuous restaurants, hotels and diner service. The typical railroad depot was of frame construction, with the Harvey House usually under the same roof. Telegrams were sent ahead from the train announcing the number of passengers who would dine. When the train pulled in a gong sounded the way. The passengers were waited on by the famed Harvey Girls, young and adventurous, intelligent and refined. The time allotted for meal stops was usually thirty minutes, but the skill with which the service was organized gave the patrons the impression of dining leisurely. The girls lived in the house in charge of a matron—but not for long. In the womanless West they were quickly snapped up, although they had promised when joining Fred Harvey not to marry for a year. Harvey's labor turnover was terrific.

In the eighties the crew of this Harvey lunchroom in Arizona looked a businesslike lot who could appreciate good eating.

As a change from dealing them off the arm, the biscuit-shooters held dances on Saturday nights and staged amateur theatricals.

They would hardly have recognized themselves in the movie Hollywood
made about them 60 years later, but their fame was secure.

In the 70's there were no vestibules at the ends of coaches and passengers remained in the car they boarded. Conductors climbed from one car to another at great risk. Diners were unheard of. Coach seats had low

backs and little padding. Trips of a few hundred miles were an ordeal, yet far easier than by any other means. In 1876 the first sleeping cars were bought from Pullman.

They were the "newest and best coaches" to be had. Oil lamps superseded candles and hot water heating replaced the old stoves.

Later was to come the dining car, a "gem of comfort." Fred Harvey, naturally, was in charge and offered his typical cuisine.

In the beginning, refined maiden ladies were not quite sure it was morally proper to travel and sleep on a train carrying persons of both sexes. This etching, published in 1875, was a subtle effort to reassure them. Under the title "Singing Hymns of a Sunday Night while Crossing the Plains," the artist portrays the two Weber organs with which these early luxury trains were equipped, and also displays the last word in ornamentation and what was then esteemed as "elegance." The woodwork and trim were of mahogany, English oak and satinwood, all elaborately inlaid—including the ceiling—and decorated with filigree and grille work. Drapes, hassocks and fancy carpets were the fashion. Note the early upper-berth sections and the reverent conductor in the far background removing his cap and joining in the singing.

175

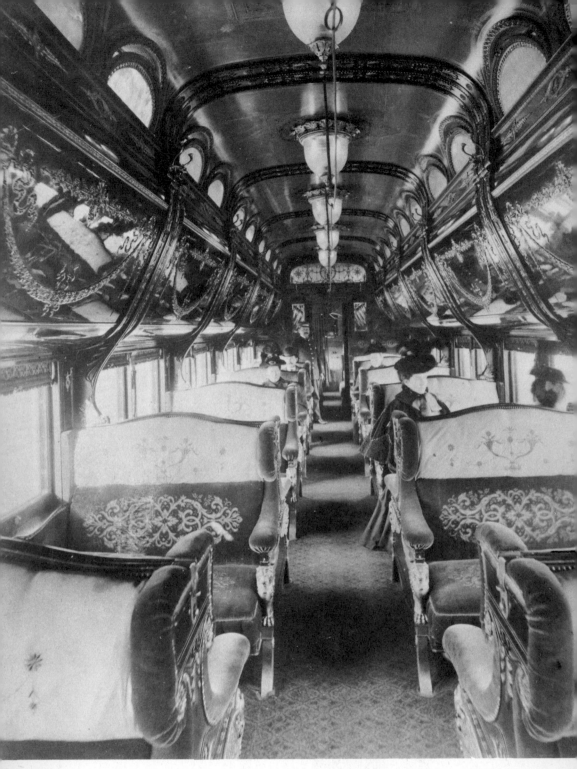

When sleeping cars were upholstered in peacock blue glacé plush in Louis XV design it looked as if the railroad had come to stay.

Ladies who had thought it hardly proper to ride in a sleeper now abandoned their misgivings. Sometimes they brought a mandolin.

Early Pullman facilities were primitive when judged by modern standards of comfort, but a covered wagon was never like this.

What? Hot and cold running water in the middle of the prairie? Things were very different when mother crossed the plains.

Where only trappers and settlers had gone, tourists now followed to see the wonders of Colorado, the "Switzerland of America."

And old folks headed for California, to spend their remaining days in the never-failing sunshine they had heard so much about.

Business boomed as traveling salesmen took to the rails. The company built new depots and freight offices, hired more hands.

There was good reason why it should, when gold miners could bring $110,000 in bullion to a station on the line in Arizona.

1870

1880

1890

1900

The progress of the railroad may be judged from these pictures of
184

locomotives taken at ten-year intervals from 1870 to 1940.

Today new 4-8-4 high-speed steam engines like this haul many Santa Fe trains on parts of the run from Chicago to the Coast and the Gulf.

This big Diesel freight locomotive, 5,400 h.p., was the first Diesel ever placed in regular main-line freight service.

This locomotive of the 3460 class hauls the Chief and other high-speed passenger trains between Chicago and La Junta.

A Diesel pulls the Super Chief in Cajon Pass, where the transcontinental trains cross the Coast Range en route to the Pacific.

CHAPTER SIX

TRANSPORTATION OPENED THE REACHES OF THE
SOUTHWEST TO COMMERCE AND INDUSTRY. THE
REGION'S ECONOMY TODAY DEPENDS ON SWIFT
SERVICE ALONG THE MODERN SANTA FE TRAIL.

THE MODERN SOUTHWEST

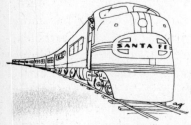

WHEN Cyrus Holliday conceived his railroad and predicted that it would eventually reach Lake Michigan, the Gulf, Santa Fe and the Pacific, he spoke of great agricultural and industrial developments to come in the region southwest of Kansas. This was remarkable foresight in its day, but even Holliday's long view fell short. If he had actually foretold what was about to take place in the Southwest and adjoining states, and had dared to expound it to his fellow citizens in Topeka, he would have risked being locked up as an old gent very wrong in the head.

The Southwest, at the time Holliday was building his road, was immense. It is still immense today. It was also deserted. In Oklahoma, Texas, New Mexico and Arizona were tremendous tracts of land inhabited only by Indian tribes and cowboys. Small towns and trading posts were scattered over the vast landscape. Indian villages existed as they had for hundreds of years. When the gold fever struck in Colorado and Arizona, shack towns sprang up overnight into gaudy cities that lived briefly and crumbled into forgetfulness. Transportation was painfully slow. But with the railroads came settlers, and with settlers came the bases of commerce and industry. Farms became accessible to distant markets; farm produce began to move swiftly and economically to centers where it could be sold profitably. More towns were laid out, and transportation, in turn, grew in importance.

The Santa Fe Trail, which had crawled 800 miles over plain and mountain to link Missouri with New Mexico, the new civilization with the old, at last extended itself to cover with steel rails more than 13,000 miles in nine States, and the Southwestern quadrant of

189

the nation leaped, in a bare half-century, into a region of fabulous riches.

The Southwest proper—Oklahoma, Texas, New Mexico and Arizona—to which the modern Santa Fe joins Kansas, Colorado and California, is an area of awesome distances, of color, of towering mountains and canyoned rivers, of natural wonders, of hogans and pueblos, of a climate that exerts a benign influence on living things. But beyond these, Nature has been bountiful here. There are oil, gold, sulfur, potash, forests, land that will grow anything, and grazing for millions of cattle and sheep.

Kansas, once the sloping bed of a shallow sea from whose rich sediment now spring her tremendous crops of hard wheat and corn, produces also more cattle than 42 other states and usually has more hogs than people. Oklahoma, a land of oil derricks and wheatfields, is young and lusty; its history has been compressed into the lifetime of many inhabitants. Texas, major producer of cotton, oil and cattle, has skyscraper cities as progressive as any in the East. Yet the frontier still exists; cattlemen drive into the cities in cars, but back home they climb aboard a horse again. Arizona contrasts arid deserts with semi-tropical irrigated valleys. Colorado is a playground, yet its mines have produced metal worth billions of dollars. And Southern California, paradise of them all, contains some of the richest agricultural land in the world and is at the same time one of the major industrial producers in the United States.

When in 1885 the Santa Fe reached Los Angeles and began its rate war with the Southern Pacific, it started what was then the greatest of the Southwest's real-estate booms. Trains rolled into Los Angeles packed to the doors with Kansas farmers, precursors of millions who were to follow in the next half-century. Ten years later an even bigger boom came when oil was discovered in California. Since 1940 there has been another great influx into the Southwest, one of the largest westward mass movements in American history. Thus the trend begun by the pioneers continues today; since gold was discovered in the Sacramento River, the West has been developed by migrants.

THE WESTERN DREAM

What is it that draws Americans westward? Tradition, perhaps; the persistent dream that when drought, depression and unemployment are felt in the East there are still opportunities in the West, that westward the land is bright. To fulfill that dream, millions have crossed the Rockies since the day the Santa Fe arrived in Los Angeles.

Given a territory rich in minerals and soil fertility and with a suitable climate, only the addition of transportation and an industrious, skilled people is necessary to create a prosperous economy. Because the Southwest has all these, its advance cannot be counted a modern miracle, but it has been swift indeed.

What has been the part of the Santa Fe in this tremendous development? William Allen White, the Emporia, Kansas, editor, had nothing but good to say of the railroad's contribution: "The Santa Fe," he wrote, "is the best thing that ever happened to Emporia. It is one of the best things that ever happened to Kansas. It is easily one of the best things that ever happened to this land."

Sixty years of migration on foot, on horseback and by wagon had settled only a few thousand people in an area about half the size of the United States. When the railroad came it often doubled and redoubled the population of great areas in a few years. In 1865 Kansas had some 140,000 people. The Santa Fe came along in 1869. By 1877 there were 700,000 in the state. The Arkansas Valley, between Hutchinson and Pueblo, Colorado, provides an even more remarkable example. Before the Santa Fe reached the valley 2,019 persons inhabited it and only 7,000 acres were tilled. In 1877 it had 67,450 inhabitants and 600,000 acres were under crop. In that same year the land office at Larned, Kansas, handed over 600,000 acres to some 5,000 settlers; in Wichita 400,000 acres went to 3,500 pioneers.

This almost unbelievable expansion is surprising enough, but there is another feature equally noteworthy. It is this: the land had been there for years, ready to be tilled. Anyone could have had it but no one wanted it. Without transportation there was no way to make a living out of it. What gave the land its new value was its sudden accessibility to distant markets to which farm products could be shipped at reasonable charges. And settlers could now afford to buy goods from the East. Freight rates by railroad were about one-third of stagecoach and freight-wagon charges. Within a few miles of a railroad track a settler could prosper; without the railroad he could only exist.

Thus it was that when the railroad came to Kansas the settlers it brought with it turned the prairie into prosperous farmland. Kansas eventually took the leadership in quantity and quality of wheat, and the breadbasket of the nation moved to the Middle West. Texas became the nation's leading producer of cotton, and it grew so luxuriantly in New Mexico and Arizona, it was said, that the pickers no longer had to stoop. By 1940, the value of farm property in the nine states served by the Santa Fe reached $19,431,000,000, slightly more than one-third the U. S. total. More than one-third of the nation's cattle were in the area. It produced nearly half the nation's mineral output, and more

191

than 80 per cent of her crude petroleum was extracted there. More than a quarter of the country's wholesale business was transacted in the nine states (only 75 years earlier their contribution had been negligible). Yet the Southwest is still relatively undeveloped.

The Southwest's great problem, except in certain wooded mountain sections, has been water. Nature's distribution has therefore had to be rearranged by irrigation systems; but man-made irrigation, though costly, makes the water supply predictable and accurately dispenses it to the needs of the crops. Thus the great Central Valley, 450 miles long, which was once a desert, now produces nearly half California's farm products. Irrigation has led to large-scale farming, highly mechanized and employing gangs of migrant workers. It has led also to specialization, for when water can be scientifically and accurately controlled, the farmer can risk all on one crop. On land that was formerly barren or suitable only for grazing, a single crop will march for miles over the fields. Near San Joaquin, California, a 200-acre ranch raises nothing but pears. A typical ranch of 6,000 acres ships more than two dozen carloads of peaches, plums and grapes daily at the season's peak and employs 2,500 men and women in orchards and packing sheds.

The Southwest has made spectacular use of water for irrigation not only in California, but in Arizona, New Mexico, Colorado and Texas as well. Arizona's valley lands have thus been made extraordinarily fertile; lettuce, citrus fruit, tomatoes, carrots, melons, cotton and even dates grow profusely. Greatest of such developments there is the Salt River Reclamation Project. Roosevelt Dam, 75 miles northeast of Phoenix, was built in 1911 to control the Salt River, which furnished an inadequate water supply to the few farmers bold enough to locate along its banks. The arid, sun-baked lands of central Arizona were transformed by its storage reservoirs into the seventh richest agricultural area in the United States. Water for the Tempe-Mesa-Chandler-Phoenix section is now derived chiefly from reservoirs of the Horse Mesa and Canyon Lake dams. Crops ripen in the Salt River Valley every month in the year. More than 1,400 miles of main and lateral canals now make it possible for some 200,000 Arizonans to operate the 10,000 farms in the valley.

In Southern Texas, the Lower Rio Grande Valley is another example. There the mesquite has been cut away and orchards of lemons, grapefruit and limes range in orderly profusion between irrigation ditches. This semi-tropical oasis, literally handmade among the desert palm trees, now supports 76 towns and a population claimed to reach 250,000.

192

But wondrous as are these examples of the use of water, there are others; harnessing of the West's inexhaustible rivers has provided inexhaustible power. Nearly three-fifths of the nation's hydroelectric output is generated by the West's turbulent rivers. The Colorado, in its onrush of 1,700 miles from the Rockies to the sea, speeds through the Southwestern states and leaves in its wake tremendous reservoirs of power and irrigation. From its descent to the Pacific, it is estimated that 6,000,000 horsepower of electrical energy some day can be obtained. Detained at the Nevada-Arizona border by Boulder Dam, a man-made barrier 726 feet high, it pauses momentarily to throw off 1,000,000 kilowatts and supply nearly half the total power consumption of Southern California. Experts believe that, with full conservation and development of the Colorado's resources, the Southwestern States can expect a ten-fold increase in population and a corresponding accretion of wealth and prosperity.

Wealth and prosperity! Never did they come so fast to man as in Oklahoma. She and her people have moved at headlong speed since the land rush of little more than half a century ago. Half of her 70,057 square miles is in farms, but what is more important to Oklahomans is not what grows on the land but what comes out of it. Oil derricks punctuate the plains and stride into the cities themselves; they even invade the lawns of the Capitol in Oklahoma City.

Yet Oklahoma's prewar yearly average of 185,293,000 barrels of crude petroleum is surpassed by both California and Texas. (Through 1945, the wells of the West had produced more than 26,000,000,000 barrels of crude, about five times as much as produced in states east of the Mississippi.)

Tulsa is the industrial capital of Oklahoma, and the state's leading industry, naturally enough, is petroleum refining. The manufacture of oil-well equipment runs second; but zinc-smelting and industries allied to her agricultural economy, such as flour-milling and meat-packing, run into impressive figures. Her farm crops repeat the roster of the other Southwestern States in a somewhat more limited range: cotton, wheat, corn, potatoes and oats; fruits, melons and sorghums. Sheep, cattle, hogs and poultry are produced in important quantity.

Oklahoma's history is compressed into a few years. She had hardly any youth; she flashed into maturity from infancy. El Reno's population, for example, leaped from 7,000 to more than 70,000 in 24 hours when the Kiowa-Comanche Reservation was thrown open in 1901 and lotteries were held for free lands. Penniless immigrants became wealthy men literally overnight. In one lifetime, Oklahoma civilization changed from that of the blanket Indian to that of the air-conditioned cocktail lounge.

But civilization struck Oklahoma only a little faster, relatively, than it did the rest of the Southwest. Colorado, New Mexico and Arizona today base their prosperity on agriculture, mining and the tourist trade. Arizonans, for instance, summarize their economic life simply by repeating a number of words beginning with C—copper, cattle, cotton, citrus, climate. Copper may well head the list, for Arizona has led the United States since 1907 in its production. She has contributed billions of pounds to the world's supply, and has many more billions of pounds yet to be extracted at a cost ranging from six to fourteen cents a pound. But not all her wealth lies in copper; she has much gold, silver and lead, and many more minerals less well known but equally essential—molybdenum, vanadium, tungsten, strontium, feldspar, manganese.

Climate, in the lexicon of Arizona and Colorado, means tourists. Arizona has built the dude-ranch fad into big business. Tucson estimates its yearly income from make-believe cowpokes at $4,000,000. The entire state profits to the extent of some $75,000,000 annually. Tucson, Phoenix, Flagstaff, Tombstone are full of wonderful characters and adjacent to exciting scenery that attracts their quota of visitors, summer and winter.

But Arizona's top-ranking attraction is one of the world's wonders —the Grand Canyon of the Colorado. It is impossible to write of the Canyon except in superlatives; those who have seen it are unable to express coherently what they have witnessed. "It seems like a gigantic statement for even Nature to make—all in one mighty stone word," said John Muir, American conservationist.

Erosion, to be prosaic about it, made the Canyon, and it took more than a million years. The Canyon, cut in a plateau that stands 5,000 to 9,000 feet above sea level, varies from four to eighteen miles wide and runs 280 miles long. At points the Colorado River lies a mile deep from the rim. The most impressively beautiful part of the gorge stands in the 56 miles of the Grand Canyon National Park established by Congress in 1919. To it have come hundreds of thousands of visitors to gaze on its ever-changing grandeur.

Although Colorado, whose southern margin is properly included in the Southwest, has no such spectacular single attraction as the Grand Canyon, it has more and higher mountains than Switzerland, and from tourists who come to camp, fish, hunt, ski and generally look around among them it takes $100,000,000 a year. It is hardly surprising that this figure represents the state's largest and most profitable business.

Mining is often presumed to be Colorado's basic industry, but agriculture produces more of her yearly income. The quantity of Colorado's agricultural products is less remarkable than their diversity. She stands first in the growing of sugar beets; her Rocky Ford cantaloupes, honeydew melons and her celery are known throughout the country. Carnations grown around Denver are shipped as far as London. A quarter of all employed Coloradans make their living by farming. Stock raising began in 1858 when a prospector turned his oxen loose near the present site of Denver. Twenty years later cowboys were riding herd on 855,000 head of cattle. Today Colorado has 1,500,000 head. Sheep were driven to her grassy flats in the early seventies and, despite opposition of cattlemen, the flocks grew to immense numbers. Today the state fattens more spring lambs than any other in the union.

Mining, which contributed much color to Colorado's early history, has thrived since the gold rush of 1859. Her mines have yielded more than $3,000,000,000, and experts believe that her mineral resources have been little more than scratched. Of more importance than Colorado's gold—which still represents one-fifth of her mined income—are molybdenum and vanadium, used in the manufacture of steel. Four-fifths of the world's supply of molybdenum and three-quarters of America's vanadium come from Colorado mines; these, together with the extraction of coal, have put steel in first place among the state's manufactured goods.

Like her northern neighbor, Colorado, New Mexico's biggest business is entertainment of visitors. Today sightseers flock to the remains of her ancient civilizations as eagerly as the Santa Fe traders took to the Trail a hundred years ago. The state is still relatively undeveloped, for the nation's needs have not made any pressing call on her resources. But she has enough coal, for example, to meet the country's requirements for centuries after more accessible supplies have been exhausted. In the Pecos Valley are valuable potash beds. The more than 40,000 farms in the state produce corn and wheat as their principal crops; potatoes, legumes and fruit grow in quantity, and sheep are the principal livestock industry.

TEXAS—GIANT AMONG STATES

Big is the word for Texas—big ranches, big deserts, big mountains, big winds, big talk and big men. Bigger than any European country with the exception of the U.S.S.R., Texas sprawls over 266,000 square miles, and her population is sprinkled over them at the rate of 23 to the square mile. Every Texan, therefore, has room to turn around in.

Texas produces more cotton, more beef, more sheep and goats than any other state and supplies 40 per cent of the nation's oil. On the coastal plains lie its four greatest cities, Houston, Dallas, Fort Worth and San Antonio. Most of its cotton and much of its oil originate in the region; and oil has made these cities boom beyond belief. Houston now threatens to outrank New Orleans as the greatest city of the South. This Texas metropolis, fifty miles from the large seaport of Galveston on the Gulf, has been made by oil and a ship channel. Its talk is of bank deposits, clearing-house receipts, oil companies and bales of cotton. To it by tank car, ship and pipeline come some 12 per cent of U. S. oil production for processing and shipment.

Nearly a third of Texas' oil wells (26,000) are in the East Texas field, brought in in 1930. This giant oil pool, 45 miles long and three to eight miles wide, lay but 3,600 feet underground and its like may never be found again.

Dallas, the second city of Texas, is the creation of cotton; a bankers' and manufacturers' town, it takes its culture seriously and is in constant rivalry with Houston as patron of arts. Both Houston and Dallas are modern American cities, brash and bustling, throwing up skyscrapers and planning for an unlimited future. San Antonio, once the historical seat of Spanish and Mexican government, tends to look backward to the past. Liberal and easygoing, it has an air of worldly wisdom that the others lack. Its leading industry is the United States Army; before the war it had the largest military garrison in the country, and in wartime its Brooks, Kelly and Randolph Fields trained fliers by the tens of thousands.

In Southern Texas lies the brush country, covered with mesquite, the home of the *vaquero* and beef-cattle. Here the King ranch with its 1,000,000 acres and 50,000 head of cattle sprawls over nine counties.

On the great plains of Southwest Texas is the finest sheep country in the United States. Here are 80 per cent of Texas' 10,000,000 sheep, and 3,000,000 goats which produce three-quarters of the nation's mohair. It is estimated that some 20,000,000 cattle, sheep and goats graze on Texas farms and ranches. Her area and regional variations in soil conditions make it possible for Texas to grow almost every crop from wheat in the North to citrus fruits in the Rio Grande Valley. She easily leads all the cotton states, and usually leads the South in corn production.

El Paso, at the extreme Western tip of Texas, likes to think there is not another city like it in the United States. It may be right; certainly the standardization that tends to afflict the American city has been rebuffed here. The visitor sees plentiful evidence of the frontier; more people carrying guns in holsters than perhaps anywhere else in the country. Pendleton trousers and cowboy hats are worn daily by many men, even in their offices. On El Paso's streets American and Mexican rub shoulders, work side by side. Even the two languages overlap. Spanish now includes such gems as *lonche* (lunch), *troca* (truck) and *sandwicheria*. Americans for their part make free use of *porque*, *hasta la vista* and *manana*. The two international bridges across the Rio Grande from El Paso to Juarez are thronged daily. In the war years El Paso became the air hub of the Southwest and thereby acquired a more cosmopolitan flavor.

CALIFORNIA—PROMISED LAND

But if Texas is big, California is fabulous. The rewards that awaited the settlers in, say, Kansas were as nothing compared to the riches Southern California had to offer. There, incomparable climate lured the newcomers, and rich land held them. It was land on which anything could grow, once water had been brought to it. And in addition to the land there was gold and oil. Between 1900 and 1940, when the population of the United States increased 73 per cent, California's population grew 365 per cent—and Southern California's more than 1,000 per cent. Los Angeles, heart and nerve center of this region, is today the third largest United States city in population; its inhabitants believe it soon will be the largest. Already it is greatest in area, with city limits as much as fifty miles apart. Where greater Los Angeles sprawls today was covered by orange groves in 1910; fifty years ago the region was a desert.

Southern California's productivity is startling. Los Angeles County is probably the richest agricultural land in the world, and agriculture, despite the new industries that have sprung up, is still the West Coast's most important business. Oranges, lemons, grapefruit, grapes, apricots, prunes, berries, figs, dates, carrots, beans, cabbage and lettuce grow in abundance. The value of these crops is higher than in any other county in the United States. In California there are 9,200,000 acres of farmland now in use and there will be many more when the Bureau of Reclamation's irrigation program has been completed. Alongside these great crops of fruit and vegetables there are palms, eucalyptus from Australia, honeysuckle, heliotropes, roses and geraniums blooming the year around; the skies are blue, the sun shines unceasingly and fall never comes. In these surroundings the people of Southern California work and play with a zest and precocity unmatched elsewhere in the country. No Americans live more out of doors and none are more affected by the climate and the variety of nature that is theirs.

Eighty per cent of Los Angeles residents were born elsewhere. To Southern California they brought energy and a restless and uninhibited temperament. The combination of a people unfettered by tradition and a climate that goes to the head has produced a rocketing economy, to which the war gave new impetus. In the five years from 1940 to

1945 more than 2,000,000 migrants entered the three West Coast States; Southern California shared with Washington and Oregon the new industrial boom. To the U. S. movie industry and the manufacture of oil-well machinery, in which the Los Angeles area was already paramount, were added the manufacture of aircraft and such new war plants as synthetic rubber, shipbuilding and steel. But even before war came Los Angeles County was a major industrial producer in its own right; it assembled more cars than any other city except Detroit, made more furniture than Grand Rapids, was the third city in food processing and packing, was third in oil refining and was fourth in the manufacture of clothing.

The war years wrought changes in the Southwest's economy that did not pass with the coming of peace; industrialization came to the Southwest in the form of heavy industry. Millions who flocked there to man war plants intend to stay, as the bulk of other migrants did before them. Where factories, machine shops and construction gangs have appeared, the Southwest has perforce turned to the new problems of industrial pioneering.

Whatever changes the Southwest faces under war-born industrialization, her people look forward to them with typical assurance, confident that whatever strains are imposed on their hitherto agricultural-mineral economy will be overcome by Western frankness, directness and energy. They recall that, less than 150 years ago, their tremendous empire where millions now live was the domain of the redman. They know that the Southwest was built by men of fortitude and initiative whose essential toughness of mind and character is present in their descendents today.

But, transcending any temporary disruption of the Southwest's economy, stands the land itself, a land of contrasts and opposites— The Grand Canyon and the Painted Desert, the Petrified Forest and the cliff dwellings, the pueblos, the Hopis, the Navajos, the shining mountains and the sunbaked plains. The velvet nights of the prairie, the stars blazing seemingly at arm's length, the life-giving sunshine; distances, colors, the play of light and shade on butte and mesa, the snow-hooded peaks a hundred miles off, the line of the horizon sharp as a knife blade, a dust storm starting up in a river bed, and over all the arc of the sky—these are the Southwest. To them were drawn the men who made her great; to them will continue to flow new streams of population, releasing new riches from her vast stores. Thus will the Southwest—old, yet young—achieve her great destiny.

As the modern traveler speeds through the Southwest, the old Santa Fe Trail flashes by, its remains noted here and there by a historical marker, a lonely stone set beside the steel rails, a mound that rises

198

abruptly above the flat plain. The Arkansas, where the wagons slid and toppled as they came to the ford, looks much like any other river when seen through windows of a club car; the fearsome Raton Pass, whose boulders and precipices were once a major barrier to the traders, is but a deep rumbling heard dimly as the Pullmans steadily mount the grade.

But for those who can recall the past as they are hurried into the future the Santa Fe Trail still lives. It exerted an extraordinary influence on the lives and thoughts of men; it carried its portion of the flow of westward expansion; and when at last its traffic fell away, its task had been accomplished. It had linked the new civilization with the old. The people who raised dust clouds along its ancient furrows had added a great territory to the United States.

Of the Trail there remained nothing but the ruts that creased the Great American Desert and the place names that were to become part of the American legend. When the men who had plodded its forbidding miles disappeared, the Trail also vanished. For what was the Trail but the pioneers who peopled it? Without men the Trail was but part of the desert; the men who made the Trail also gave it life and significance. It is these men and their deeds that the traveler remembers today. Today the Trail is synonymous with adventure, progress and the imponderable aspirations of men's minds and hearts.

Kansas City, where the Missouri River sweeps in from the north and turns east, is the main gateway to the Southwest today. Here the early immigrants disembarked to proceed overland by pack mule and Conestoga wagon; here today steel rails mark the beginning of the modern Santa Fe Trail. Kansas Citians like to say that if a freight car

were taken a couple of hundred miles to the north, west or southwest and given a shove, it would coast down to Kansas City. However that may be, they have seized on the city's strategic location, and twelve trunk-line railways now use the Union Station (above), one of the five largest rail terminals in the world.

Near Kansas City, streamliners flash across the Missouri River . . .

. . . speeding their passengers in comfort toward the plains . . .

. . . where the 5,400-h. p. Diesels touch close to 100 m. p. h.

Today Kansas means wheat. Ranking fourth in production of food crops, her fertile acres have yielded as much as 250,000,000 bushels of

hard winter wheat in a single season. Kansas uses more wheat just for seed than the total harvested in 28 other states.

In fact, Kansas consistently grows more than half of all hard wheat produced in the United States. Kansas is first, too, in flour-milling, but is far from having a one-crop economy.

She has more acres devoted to corn than have 33 other states. The seasonal stream of grains from her rich soil helps set her total farm income above that of three-fourths of all other states.

Wheat and oil spring out of the same earth in the Trapp Field near

But livestock, not crops, is chief source of Kansas farm income. The Kansas City stockyards can handle 175,000 animals daily.

Susank, Kansas. There are nearly 150 wells in this pool.

Not all of Kansas cattle are beef animals like the above. She has an average annual dairy production of some $30,000,000.

The arms of the Old Santa Fe Trail crossed from Kansas into Colorado; now signal towers flash messages to Santa Fe trains . . .

. . . carrying passengers and freight in safety and comfort along the route where once prairie schooners lurched westward.

Scenic beauty that impressed the early emigrants is still present to delight the modern traveler. Here the line snakes over Raton Pass, where the traders struggled with their teams and wagons to surmount the barrier and where Dick Wootton built his toll road.

Denver, Colorado's capital, is the gateway to the Rocky Mountain
National Park, and gold was once mined a few miles outside of the
city. These two facts are the key to much of the State's prosperity;
tourists leave behind them $100,000,000 annually, and Colorado's
mines have yielded more than $3,000,000,000.

212

But agriculture is Colorado's leading industry, producing more of her yearly income than do her mines. A quarter of the state's employed inhabitants earn their living in stock-raising and dairy-farming. Today Colorado fattens more spring lambs than any other state in the Union.

The Cliff Dwellers built these aboriginal apartment houses around 1100 A. D. Some of the finest examples of cliff dwellings in America are to be found in the Mesa Verde National Park in Southern Colorado.

The "playground of America" provides excellent sports the year round, among them skiing, as here within a few hours' drive of Denver.

Colorado is the vacationist's paradise. Mountains, forests and lakes crowd her 66 million acres. She has 47 peaks more than 14,000 feet high; Switzerland has but nine. The Rocky Mountain and Mesa Verde national parks attract thousands of visitors yearly, as do Pike's Peak and the Colorado Springs area. Some of the finest fishing in America is to be had in Colorado and the hunter finds big game plentiful.

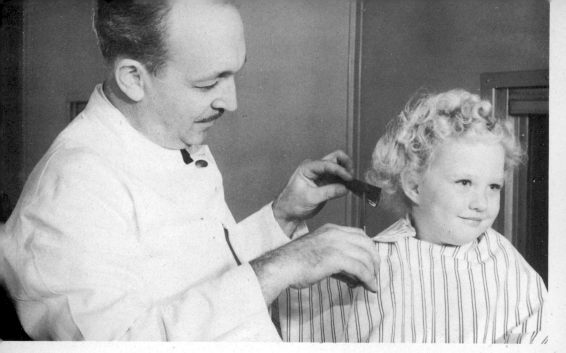

Modern train travel along the Santa Fe Trail offers luxuries undreamed of by the pioneers: up-to-date barber service . . .

. . . games and recreation. Early traders, unlike these travelers, rested only when they reached the journey's end.

Oklahoma, of wheatfields, oil derricks and industry, draws her wealth almost equally from these three. The state has also made use of extensive water-power resources. Above is the Grand River Dam, greatest multiple-arch dam in the world, capable of developing 200,000,000 kilowatts of power annually.

Derricks surround the State Capitol at Oklahoma City, all but encroaching on its lawns. Geologists estimate there are still tremendous oil resources in the state.

But Oklahoma is not all oil. This Tulsa rose garden, as incongruous as an oil derrick in England, is one of the manmade beauty spots that lend charm to the state.

Midwest City, a wartime housing development with modern planning and eighteen types of architecture, contrasts sharply with the bare

plains that were opened to the settlers in the Oklahoma land rush little more than half a century ago.

Counterpart of the traders' camps where pack mules and oxen were fed, watered and rested are the modern Santa Fe Trail's railroad yards where locomotives and rolling stock get attentive care. Filling this locomotive's sand dome will provide better traction for the long run across the plains, the pull up mountains beyond.

To many Americans, Texas means cattle—and it has a normal supply of some 7,000,000 head, nearly a tenth of the U. S. total.

Some of the finest horses in the country come from the round-ups on the vast ranches that sprawl across Texas' Southern tip.

But the state is not all cattle and cowboys. Parts of Texas are as fast in tempo as Manhattan. Houston and Dallas pride themselves on their progressiveness, their modern stores and office blocks, their opera seasons and their symphony orchestras. Even San Antonio, that tends to look backward to a historic past, is a modern city, as this view of its post office building shows.

225

Petroleum lifted Texas from industrial insignificance. Forty per cent of the nation's oil comes from the fields in her coastal plains, and oil supports half the population, directly or indirectly. In wartime, three hundred thousand barrels of Texas oil flowed daily by pipeline as

far as New Jersey, 1,362 miles away. By tanker it goes to all parts
of the world. Such big expansion tanks as these at Borger have become
as much a part of the Texas scene as a cattle round-up.

227

Magic Valley, on the Lower Rio Grande, is Texas' main producer of fruit and vegetables. Irrigation has transformed what was a barren land of mesquite and tumbleweed into a semi-tropical oasis. Grapefruit and orange orchards are laid out with precision and palm trees line the roadways. A paved highway, called by the inhabitants the longest street in America, links many valley communities. The citrus crop used to be packed in boxes and baskets for shipment; now vast juicing and canning plants have combined industry with agriculture, and the consumption of the crop has been multiplied many times. About $120,000,000 of citrus products from the valley are sold annually. Some orchardists net as high as $1,000 an acre per year. One housewife is reputed to have earned $210 from the fruit on two grapefruit trees in her front yard. At the canning plants the fruit is dumped on conveyers; shortly another moving belt carries the pasteurized juice, canned, labeled and cartoned, into waiting freight cars.

228

"Remember the Alamo!" still rings in the hearts of Texans. The symbol of the state's fight for independence from Mexico stands as it did in 1836 when every defender died within its walls. Today, scarred by the passage of time, it is surrounded by modern business blocks.

Dallas is proud of one of the world's most fashionable stores, Neiman-Marcus. More exclusively designed clothes are sold here than in any other store in the U. S. The wives of wealthy oil and cattlemen throng its elegant salons to buy its own creations and those of Hattie Carnegie, Adrian, Lily Dache, John-Frederics and others. Here one of its frequent style shows is under way.

Downtown Houston is representative of Texas' busy, metropolitan life.

The San Antonio symphony orchestra performs on its river-bank stage.

231

Galveston, on the Gulf of Mexico, is separated from the mainland by
Galveston Bay. One of the world's great seaports, from which some

60 steamship lines operate, the city is a leading exporter of cotton, grain and flour.

Industry in Texas hinges on its vast supply of raw materials. Oil, of course, stands in the forefront; but her second greatest mineral resource is sulphur, and out of her vast deposits she produces about three-quarters of the nation's total supply.

Crop-farming and stock-raising on the 137,600,000 acres owned by farmers are enormous industries. Annual cash farm income runs into more than $1,200,000,000. Cotton is the greatest crop, so much so that Texas far out-produces any other state.

Playing its part in the Southwest's swift transport, this centralized traffic-control board throws switches 75 miles away . . .

. . . keeps trains moving by cutting waiting time to a minimum. Aboard the Santa Fe's Chief, passengers dine in air-cooled comfort.

Maintenance work goes on constantly. Here an inspector checks the voltage on the lamp of a searchlight bridge signal.

Change comes slowly to New Mexico. The Plaza in Santa Fe is not much altered since trading days; if anything, it is more deserted now.

The Southwest's scenery and colors make it a painter's paradise. At Taos, New Mexico, there is an important art colony.

New Mexico, dreaming in the sun about its romantic past, provides fascinating glimpses of Indian festivals and ceremonies.

Within their life span, older Indians of New Mexico have seen their lands invaded by the white man, their lives and habits challenged by a new civilization. But the Indians have clung tenaciously to their tribal customs, and the elders, like the Zuni above seen drilling a turquoise, hand on their legends and rites to their grandchildren.

240

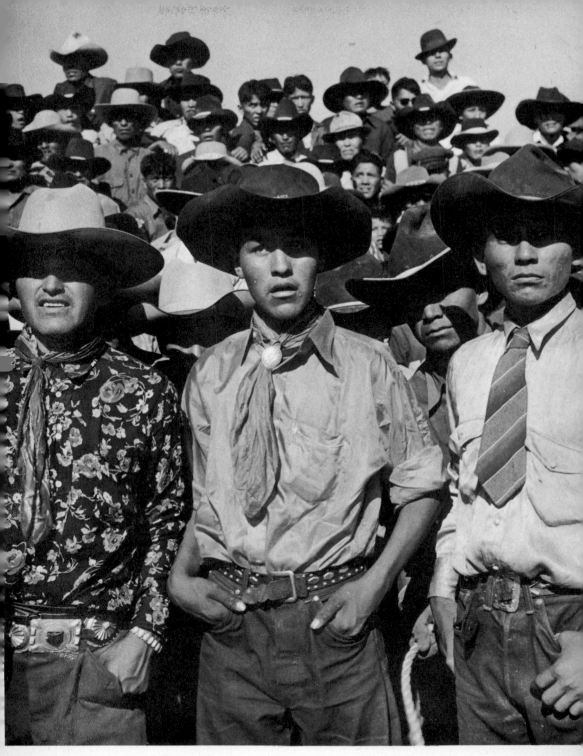

In bright-colored velveteen shirts, their leather belts lavishly adorned with silver and wearing levis and Stetsons, trade-marks of the white cowboy, these Navajos of the new generation watch a rodeo.

Not all of New Mexico's scenic beauty is above ground. Carlsbad Caverns, in the southeastern desert country, are fantastic in their shapes and colors. These subterranean chambers have been formed through millions of years by the action of water seeping through limestone. Discovered in 1901, their countless rooms have been explored since then, and today the caverns are a national park.

In the Cimarron Valley corn and wheat are the principal crops.

In Arizona the Canyon Diablo bridge, over which early Santa Fe trains crawled with a six-car drag, now carries streamliners.

243

Arizona's Boulder Dam (above) shares with Grand Coulee in Washington the distinction of being the greatest water and power project ever undertaken. Completed in 1936, it cost $125,000,000; its power plant generates 1,000,000 kilowatts, supplies Southern California.

This once-arid section in the Salt River Valley, with year-round sunshine and fertile soil, has been made productive by irrigation. Off-season crops, like the winter lettuce shown here, help supply the nation's markets. War veterans have settlement priority in the project.

Indian handicrafts are a steady source of interest to tourists.

The rodeo is to Arizona what baseball is to the nation.

Arizona, too, has its ruins of ancient cultures. Montezuma Castle, 55 miles from Prescott, was abandoned around 1400 when warfare, starvation and disease are thought to have forced Indian inhabitants to move. Sightseers by thousands now visit the spot.

This open pit of an Arizona copper mine helps to explain why the State leads in copper production. But not all her mineral wealth is in copper; she has gold, silver and lead as well.

248

These date-bearing palms in the Salt River Valley are standing in irrigation water. About three such floodings equal a year's rainfall in Southwest Arizona. Nearly all dates grown in the United States come from irrigation projects like this in the Southwest.

Near Flagstaff, Arizona, today's Santa Fe Trail passes majestic scenery. In the background the San Francisco Peaks rise to nearly 13,000 feet, Arizona's highest point.

Modern is the word for travel along today's Santa Fe Trail. Here a registered nurse looks after needs of young passengers.

Eight hundred miles out of Independence, Missouri, the old Trail came to an end in Santa Fe. It had writhed its way painfully along the Arkansas, through the mountains of Colorado or by the Cimarron cutoff. Behind it lay the landmarks that were to become legendary— Willow Springs, Council Grove, Pawnee Rock, Bent's Fort, the Raton Pass, Willow Bar, Wagon Mound. Today the steel trail projects beyond the dreams of the traders. It covers the road to Santa Fe in a swift leap and sweeps onward to the Pacific. From Arizona it speeds into California, fabulous land of gold, oil, unsurpassed fertility—and movies.

Sublime and remote, the white peak of Mount Shasta, in the Sacramento Valley, dominates the California landscape for hundreds of miles. It

stands in a region of forests, rivers, lakes and waterfalls—a natural wonderland. Yet Shasta, at 14,162 feet, is but sixth highest in the state.

Steel is California's newest industry. This blast furnace, near Fontana, has a daily capacity of 1,200 tons. With its open hearth furnaces, it turns Western ore, coal and limestone into finished steel—something that Westerners have long wanted. Despite this new industry, however, and the importance of its oil and minerals, California's main source of income is agriculture; it far outstrips oil and mining combined in dollar value of its output, and its production costs are more than three times those of the movie industry. California's de luxe fruits, vegetables and nuts are sold throughout the world.

254

More than half a million of California's sunny acres are devoted to the growing of grapes. Here, Red Malagas, a table grape, are picked in a Kern County vineyard.

From her land comes wine, measured in millions of gallons.

From her seas, California takes tuna by the shipload.

In the Sacramento-San Joaquin Valley, called the world's most fertile growing region, an army of migrant workers harvests the great citrus crop. California's orange groves lured thousands of settlers and are now a conspicuous part of her scenery.

258

The redwoods, probably the oldest living things in the world, are found in the Sierra Nevadas and the Coast Range. Some of them are at least 4,000 years old. Founder's Grove, shown here, contains the world's tallest tree, 364 feet in height and 47 feet in circumference.

California is a playground for millions. Her beaches . . .

. . the scenic beauty of her desert country . . .

. . . the deep and satisfying silences of her streams and mountains offer the vacationist a variety perhaps not found anywhere else in such proximity. From beach cabana to mountain lodge is but overnight; a day's drive from Los Angeles takes the motorist into a year-round wonderland of winter sports on snow-clad peaks.

Palomar Observatory, 50 miles north of San Diego, will be the world's largest when it is completed with the installation of a 200-inch mirror. It was constructed at a cost of $6,000,000, and is typical, perhaps, of California's predilection not merely for what is biggest or most expensive, but for what is best.

The state is equally proud of her schools and colleges, her colonies of musicians, artists and intellectuals.

The symphony orchestras of the West Coast have played under the world's great conductors. Above is a Hollywood Bowl performance.

California has Hollywood; and Hollywood is practically all of the U. S. movie industry, which spends around $300,000,000 yearly on making motion pictures. Here, a camera crew films a scene for one of the 350 pictures Hollywood produces each year to draw the staggering total of 4,940,000,000 admissions to American movie theaters. Hollywood probably commands more genius among its people than any other city; it also has perhaps more freaks, dreamers and hangers-on.

The film industry takes itself with great seriousness, plays its premieres straight, with the decorum of a high-class funeral.

The rewards of successful movie-making are great. Such lush surroundings as the above are a part of the Hollywood colony.

265

The modern Sante Fe Trail ends at Los Angeles (above), San Diego and San Francisco. Perhaps that is poetic justice. The gold-rush days had passed the old Trail by, and it languished and lingered on while California lived through its most exciting era. But at length the steel rails crept high into the Rockies, over the Sierras, the Sangre de Cristos and the Glorietas, to come at last to the Pacific. The Santa Fe Railroad, on its way to Los Angeles, threw steel from Illinois to the Western

ocean, bridged the Mississippi, the Missouri, the Canadian, the Colorado, the Red, the Cimarron, the Illinois, the Des Moines. On its way it left behind shacks that were to grow into hamlets, hamlets into towns and towns into cities. As it advanced it brought people with it, gave them the transportation they needed to develop the region we now call the Southwest. By their vision and their industry, those people made the Southwest great.

ACKNOWLEDGMENTS

For assistance in preparing this book we express gratitude to Dr. L. L. Waters of the University of Kansas; James Marshall, author of *Santa Fe, the Railroad that Built an Empire;* Dorothy W. Estes, director of the San Jacinto Museum of History Association; Dr. and Mrs. Herbert Gambrell of the Dallas Historical Society; Helen M. McFarland, librarian of the Kansas State Historical Society; Hirst Milhollen and Milton Kaplan of the Photographic Division, Library of Congress; Josephine Cobb, chief of research, Camilla Painter and Mrs. H. M. Baumhofer, Division of Photographic Archives, the National Archives, Washington; Romana Javitz, superintendent of the Picture Collection, New York Public Library; Cecil Howes of the Kansas City *Star;* James R. Record, managing editor of the Fort Worth *Star-Telegram;* E. M. (Ted) Dealey, president, and H. C. Withers, managing editor of the Dallas *News;* the staff and files of *The Santa Fe Magazine* and many officers and employees of the Santa Fe System Lines.

The Editors of *Look*

PICTURE CREDITS

271

a LOOK
PICTURE
BOOK